Three Sisters from the South

A Collection of Recipes by
Patsy Nichols Pomeroy, Joan Nichols Johnson, and Connie Nichols Cullers
2411 63rd Street West
Bradenton, Florida 34209

Copyright © 2008
Morris Press Cookbooks

All rights reserved. Reproduction in whole or in part without written permission is prohibited.

Printed in the U.S.A. by

Morris Press Cookbooks
P.O. Box 2110 • Kearney, NE 68848
800-445-6621 • www.morriscookbooks.com

Thank You

I wish to thank my sisters for taking the time to type and send me their favorite recipes. Thank you also to Allison Dickey for her help in proofing and organizing the cookbook.

I hope everyone enjoys our family favorites. As we would say in the south, "this food is not only good to eat, it is good for the soul."

Enjoy!

Patsy Pomeroy

Dedication

We wish to dedicate this cookbook to our mother, Lucille McKnight Nichols, now deceased, who passed on her gift of cooking to her three daughters.

Table of Contents

Appetizers & Beverages 1

Soups & Salads 13

Vegetables
   & Side Dishes 23

Main Dishes 33

Breads & Rolls 51

Desserts 59

Cookies & Candy 83

This & That 101

Family Holiday Meals

Index

Appetizers & Beverages

Helpful Hints

- Add flavor to tea by dissolving old-fashioned lemon drops or hard mint candies in it. They melt quickly and keep the tea brisk.

- Make your own spiced tea or cider. Place orange peels, whole cloves, and cinnamon sticks in a 6-inch square piece of cheesecloth. Gather the corners and tie with a string. Steep in hot cider or tea for 10 minutes; steep longer if you want a stronger flavor.

- Always chill juices or sodas before adding them to beverage recipes.

- Calorie-free club soda adds sparkle to iced fruit juices and reduces calories per portion.

- To cool your punch, float an ice ring made from the punch rather than using ice cubes. It appears more decorative, prevents diluting, and does not melt as quickly.

- Place fresh or dried mint in the bottom of a cup of hot chocolate for a cool and refreshing taste.

- When making fresh lemonade or orange juice, one lemon yields about ¼ cup juice, while one orange yields about ⅓ cup juice.

- Never boil coffee; it brings out acids and causes a bitter taste. Store ground coffee in the refrigerator or freezer to keep it fresh.

- Always use cold water for electric drip coffee makers. Use 1–2 tablespoons ground coffee for each cup of water.

- How many appetizers should you prepare? Allow 4–6 appetizers per guest if a meal quickly follows. If a late meal is planned, allow 6–8 appetizers per guest. If no meal follows, allow 8–10 pieces per guest.

- If serving appetizers buffet-style or seating is limited, consider no-mess finger foods that don't require utensils to eat.

- Think "outside the bowl." Choose brightly-colored bowls to set off dips or get creative with hollowed-out loaves of bread, bell peppers, heads of cabbage, or winter squash.

- Cheeses should be served at room temperature – approximately 70°.

- To keep appetizers hot, make sure you have enough oven space and warming plates to maintain their temperature.

- To keep appetizers cold, set bowls on top of ice or rotate bowls of dips from the fridge every hour or as needed.

Appetizers & Beverages

Hot Artichoke Dip

1 can artichoke hearts
1 c. grated Parmesan cheese
1 c. real mayonnaise
1 green onion, chopped thin
1 dash garlic powder

Drain artichokes, mix ingredients. Bake at 350° for 25 to 30 minutes. Serve with crackers.

Patsy Pomeroy

Bacon Wraps

1 c. grated Parmesan cheese
2 tsp. garlic salt or powder
12 slices bacon
24 (4½-inch) sesame breadsticks

Preheat oven to 350°. Mix Parmesan cheese with garlic salt or powder in a shallow dish and set aside. Cut the slices of bacon in half so that each is approximately 5 inches long. Wrap one piece of bacon around a breadstick starting at one end of breadstick and finishing at the other end. Place on a cookie sheet lined with parchment paper. Repeat this process using all of the breadsticks. Bake for approximately 15 minutes or until bacon is browned. Remove from cookie sheet and immediately roll bacon wraps in cheese mixture. Let cool and serve at room temperature. Makes 2 dozen.

Patsy Pomeroy

Praline-Topped Brie

1 (13- to 15-oz.) round Brie cheese
½ c. orange marmalade
⅓ c. chopped pecans
2 T. brown sugar

Preheat oven to 350°. Place cheese in a shallow baking dish or pie plate. In a small bowl stir together the marmalade and brown sugar.

(continued)

Spread over top of cheese, sprinkle with pecans. Bake for about 15 minutes for smaller round of cheese or 20 minutes for larger round until slightly softened and topping is bubbly. Serve with crackers.

Patsy Pomeroy

Southern Caviar

1 (10-oz.) can black-eyed peas, drained
2-4 sm. white onions, sliced thin into rings
½ tsp. Tabasco sauce
½ tsp. black pepper
⅓ jar capers, drained
1 tsp. minced garlic
⅓ bottle Italian dressing

Mix all ingredients. Refrigerate for at least 24 hours stirring occasionally. Drain. Serve with salt free crackers or pita chips.

Patsy Pomeroy

Cheese Ball

1 lg. pkg. Philadelphia cream cheese
1 Cracker Barrel sharp cheddar cheese
Juice of ¼ onion
Juice of toe of garlic
2½ T. mayonnaise
1 tsp. Worcestershire sauce
½ c. chopped nuts
2 T. chopped parsley

Blend together cream and cheddar cheeses. Add mayonnaise and Worcestershire sauce. Mix well and add juice of garlic and onion. Press into ball and roll in nuts and parsley. Place in refrigerator to set. Serve with crackers.

Patsy Pomeroy

Olive Cheese Balls

3 c. sharp cheddar cheese
½ c. plus 1 T. butter
1½ c. flour
¾ T. salt
1½ T. paprika
Sm. pimento stuffed green olives

Combine all ingredients except olives. Mix well and chill. Take a small amount of cheese mixture and press it around an olive making a small ball. Bake at 400° for 10 minutes on an ungreased cookie sheet.

Patsy Pomeroy

Hot Chipped Beef Dip

8 oz. cream cheese
1 jar or sm. pkg. chipped beef, cut fine
2 tsp. green onion, cut fine
¼ tsp. garlic salt
½ c. sour cream
3 tsp. milk
¼ tsp. pepper

Soften cream cheese then combine remaining ingredients with cheese. Put in baking dish and bake at 350° for 20 minutes. Serve with crackers.

Patsy Pomeroy

Saucy Crab Ball

1 (4½-oz.) can lump crab meat, drained
1 (8-oz.) pkg. cream cheese
⅔ c. chili sauce
Assorted crackers

Reserve a few crab lumps for garnish. Gently combine remainder of crab meat with cream cheese. Form into a ball on serving plate. Spoon chili sauce over top. Garnish with reserved crab. Serve with crackers.

Joan Johnson

Crabby Club Pizzettas

1 pkg. Louis Kemp crab delights
1 pkg. (16) Rhodes white rolls
¼ c. Alfredo pasta sauce
8 strips bacon, cooked & crumbled
½ c. diced tomato
2 c. salad greens, chopped
Ranch dressing

Thaw rolls according to directions. Flatten rolls into 5-inch mini pizza crusts. Place on lightly greased baking sheet. Top each crust with 2 teaspoons Alfredo sauce, leaving ¼ inch around crust. Add 2-3 pieces of crab meat slightly shredded, 1 tablespoon of cheese and 1 teaspoon bacon. Bake at 400° for 10 to 12 minutes until golden brown. Serve pizzettas topped with diced tomato and dressed lettuce. Makes 16.

Joan Johnson

CRABMEAT CANAPES

1 jar Old English cheese spread
1½ tsp. garlic salt
1 T. Miracle Whip
1 stick butter, softened
½ lb. fresh crab meat
1 pkg. English muffins

Mix first 5 ingredients together. Cut English muffins in halves and spread crabmeat mixture over top of muffins. Broil for 10-15 minutes.

Joan Johnson

DEVILED CRAB

2 lbs. crab meat
2 c. chopped celery
1 lg. green pepper, chopped
1 lg. onion, chopped
½ c. heavy cream
¾ c. butter
5 eggs
1 loaf French bread, toasted & crumbled
2 T. Worcestershire sauce
1 T. dry mustard
1 tsp. salt
2 tsp. lemon juice
1 dash cayenne & black pepper
1 dash thyme & pepper sauce to taste

Combine crab meat, crumbs and eggs. Mix well. Melt butter in fry pan, add green pepper, onion and celery; sauté until tender. Combine the crab meat mixture. Add cream and mix. Add all other ingredients. Place in slightly greased crab shells and top with butter. Bake in moderate oven, 350°, for 30 to 40 minutes. Makes 16 servings.

Joan Johnson

PEGGY'S CRAB SPREAD

1 lg. pkg. cream cheese, softened
1 can crab meat
1 bottle chili sauce

Spread cream cheese on dish. Top with chili sauce. Sprinkle crab meat on top. Serve with crackers.

Patsy Pomeroy

Guacamole Dip

2 (15- to 16-oz.) cans refried beans
1 (4-oz.) can chopped green chilies, undrained
1 (16-oz.) ctn. sour cream
1 pkg. taco seasoning mix
3 ripe avocados, pitted & peeled
2 T. ReaLime lime juice from concentrate or ReaLemon lemon juice from concentrate
1/2 tsp. seasoned salt
1/8 tsp. garlic salt
Shredded cheddar or Monterey Jack cheese
Chopped tomatoes
Sliced green onions
Sliced rip olives

In a small bowl combine refried beans and chilies; spread on large serving plate. Combine sour cream and taco seasoning; spoon over entire bean mixture, spreading evenly. In a small bowl mash avocados; stir in ReaLime brand and salts; spread evenly over entire sour cream mixture. Cover; chill for several hours. Just before serving garnish with cheese, tomatoes, green onions and olives. Serve with tortilla chips. Refrigerate leftovers.

Joan Johnson

Italian Squares

1/4 lb. provolone, sliced thin
1/4 lb. Swiss cheese, sliced thin
1/4 lb. boiled ham, sliced thin
1/4 lb. cooked salami, sliced thin
1/4 lb. pepperoni (opt.)
3 lg. eggs
1 sm. jar roasted peppers
1 sm. can black olives, sliced
2 pkgs. crescent rolls

Roll out one package crescent rolls on bottom of 9 x 13-inch pan. Beat eggs and brush a small amount over the rolls. Bake at 350° for about five minutes. Remove from oven and layer meat and cheese, then peppers and olives over the rolls. Pour remaining beaten egg over the meat, cheese, etc. Roll out second package of rolls and place on top. Return to oven for 30 minutes. Let rest before slicing into small squares.

Patsy Pomeroy

Swedish Meatballs

1 1/2 lbs. hamburger meat
1/2 c. milk
4 slices white bread
1 dash Tabasco sauce
Salt and pepper

(continued)

Mash up and mix together well. Make small balls. Put 1 stick margarine in large skillet and add 1 tablespoon garlic powder; brown meat all over, remove any grease. Mix in a bowl:

1 c. catsup	3 T. chopped onions
½ c. Worcestershire sauce	1 T. sugar

Place meatballs in crockpot and pour sauce over meatballs.

Joan Johnson

Cocktail Sausage in Sauce

1 jar thick Bar B Que sauce	½ c. grape jelly
½ c. chopped onion	Garlic to season
½ c. ketchup	1 pkg. little smokies sausage

Mix all ingredients together. Place sausage in crockpot, pour mixed ingredients over the sausage and marinate.

Joan Johnson

Sausage Stuffed Mushrooms

24 lg. fresh mushrooms	1 lb. hot sausage meat
1 T. butter	½ c. unseasoned bread crumbs
¼ c. oil	1 egg
1 onion, chopped	Salt and pepper to taste

Separate mushroom caps and stems. Chop stems and brown with butter. Add oil, onions and sausage. Mix in bread crumbs and egg. Add salt and pepper to taste. Stuff mixture into mushroom caps. Heat in 300° oven for 15 to 20 minutes.

Patsy Pomeroy

Mary's Sassy Salsa

Finely dice:

1 red pepper	1 onion
1 green pepper	1 jalapeño pepper
1 yellow pepper	4 banana peppers

Drain:

(continued)

1 (15-oz.) can yellow corn
1 can black beans, rinsed
1 box frozen peas, thawed
1 can diced tomatoes with
  garlic & oregano
1 jar Kraft Seven Seas Viva
  Robust Italian dressing

Mix all ingredients together and let sit for awhile before serving.

Patsy Pomeroy

Barbeque Shrimp

Mix together:

4 sticks margarine
½ tsp. cayenne pepper
2 T. garlic powder
2 T. barbecue seasoning
1 T. pepper
3 T. Worcestershire sauce
2 tsp. paprika

Peel shrimp, sauté in the mixture on range top.

Joan Johnson

Boiled Shrimp

2 lbs. fresh shrimp
Salt and pepper to taste
Cocktail sauce

Preheat a large pot with lid on medium-high heat for a few minutes. Wash shrimp well and place in pot and cover with lid. Turn heat down to simmer. Heat for 10 minutes without opening lid. After 10 minutes open lid and stir shrimp. Put lid back on and let simmer another 10 minutes. The shrimp will cook in it's own juices. With slotted ladle remove shrimp from juice and place in a large bowl. Salt and pepper to taste. Serve with cocktail sauce.

Patsy Pomeroy

Marinated Shrimp

1 lb. shrimp
1 lg. jar whole mushrooms
Small amount of snow peas
1 sm. can black olives

Mix:

(continued)

1 tsp. sugar
¼ c. sesame oil
1 clove garlic, crushed
4 strips bacon, cooked crispy
2 tsp. parsley
2 tsp. chives

Mix together and pour over shrimp, mushrooms, snow peas and olives. Refrigerate for 24 hours.

Connie Cullers

SPINACH DIP IN CABBAGE

3 (10-oz.) pkgs. frozen chopped spinach
1 c. chopped green onion
1 (16-oz.) ctn. sour cream
2 c. mayonnaise
1 lg. red cabbage
2 tsp. herb-seasoned salt
1½ tsp. oregano
1 tsp. dill weed
Juice of 1 lemon

Cook spinach according to package directions; drain well and stir in next 7 ingredients. Chill. Trim core end of cabbage to form a flat base. Cut a crosswise slice from the top making it wide enough to remove about a fourth of the head; then lift out enough inner leaves from the cabbage to form a shell about 1-inch thick. Spoon dip into cavity of cabbage and serve with an assortment of fresh vegetables.

Patsy Pomeroy

SPINACH DIP

1 pkt. Campbell's dry vegetable or onion soup & recipe mix
1 c. sour cream
1 c. plain yogurt
⅓ chopped green onions
1 pkg. frozen chopped spinach

In a bowl blend 1 pouch Campbell's dry vegetable or onion soup and recipe mix, 1 cup sour cream, 1 cup plain yogurt, ⅓ cup chopped green onions and 1 (10-ounce) package frozen chopped spinach, thawed and well drained. Cover and refrigerate for at least 2 hours.

Joan Johnson

TACO DIP

1 lb. ground beef
1 sm. onion, cut up
1 (8-oz.) ctn. sour cream
Black olives
A little chopped tomatoes
1 pkg. taco seasoning mix
1 jar salsa
1 pkg. shredded cheddar cheese

(continued)

Mix salsa and sour cream together. Brown ground beef and drain. Layer beef, sour cream mixture and top with cheddar cheese. Place sliced black olives and chopped tomatoes on top.

Connie Cullers

Banana Gone Bad Smoothie

Peel the bananas and freeze in a plastic freezer bag. In a blender mix:

1 frozen banana
½ c. vanilla yogurt
½ frozen strawberries
1 T. fresh orange juice
1 T. honey

Blend all ingredients in blender until smooth. Makes 2 cups.

Patsy Pomeroy

Hot Buttered Rum

¼ c. butter, softened
⅓ c. dark brown sugar
¼ tsp. nutmeg, freshly grated
6 whole cloves
Boiling water
Rum

Mix together butter and sugar. Add nutmeg and mix well. Into preheated mug place a dollop of mixture and top with a whole clove. Pour in 1 jigger of boiling water and 1 jigger of rum. Stir well.

Patsy Pomeroy

Bloody Mary

1½ oz. vodka
2½ oz. tomato juice
2½ oz. Campbell's beef bouillon soup
5 shakes salt
4 shakes celery salt
1 shake onion salt
1 shake garlic salt
1 shake black pepper
1 tsp. Worcestershire sauce

Mix all ingredients together and garnish with ¼ lime and stick of celery.

Patsy Pomeroy

CHAMPAGNE PUNCH

2 c. vodka, chilled
1 qt. apricot brandy, chilled
3 qt. ginger ale, chilled
4 bottles champagne, chilled
2 lemons, thinly sliced
4 oranges, thinly sliced

Pour all the ingredients into a punch bowl. Float fruit slices on top. Stir gently until well chilled. Yields 50 champagne glass-size servings.

Patsy Pomeroy

FRUIT SLUSH

1 lg. can frozen orange juice concentrate
1 lg. can crushed pineapple with juice
2 lg. pkgs. strawberries, thawed
1 lg. can water
4 oranges, cut up & seeded
1 c. sugar

Combine all ingredients in large blender along with ice cubes. Blend together to make a slush.

Joan Johnson

SPICED MOCHA MIX

1 c. nondairy creamer
1 c. hot cocoa mix
2/3 c. instant coffee powder
1/2 c. sugar
1/2 tsp. ground cinnamon
1/2 tsp. ground nutmeg

Mix all ingredients. To serve, use 3-4 heaping teaspoons with 6 ounces boiling water.

Patsy Pomeroy

ORANGE DRINK

1 1/2 (6-oz.) cans frozen orange juice concentrate
1/2 c. milk
Ice cubes
1 1/2 tsp. vanilla
1 1/2 c. water
3/4 c. sugar

Combine all ingredients in blender, cover and blend until smooth. Serve immediately.

Joan Johnson

Gala Punch

1 can Bacardi Fuzzy Naval frozen concentrate
1 (2-L.) bottle ginger ale

Mix together, serve in punch bowl and float ice ring on top.

Patsy Pomeroy

Hot Cider Punch

1½ cranberry juice
2 bottles apple cider
4 cinnamon sticks
1 tsp. whole cloves
½ c. dark brown sugar

In percolator or large pot pour cranberry juice and apple cider. In brewing basket or cheesecloth put cinnamon sticks, cloves and brown sugar. Pour when hot and ready to serve.

Patsy Pomeroy

Blonde Sangria

1 seedless orange, thinly sliced
1 lime, thinly sliced
2 T. sugar
⅓ c. orange-flavored liqueur
⅓ c. brandy
1 bottle dry white wine, chilled
2 c. club soda, chilled

Combine first five ingredients and cover; let stand at room temperature for several hours. Refrigerate mixture for up to 24 hours. Before serving add chilled wine and club soda. Stir and serve over ice

Patsy Pomeroy

Wassail

6 c. apple juice or cider
1 cinnamon stick
¼ tsp. nutmeg
½ c. honey
3 T. lemon juice
1 tsp. grated lemon peel
1 (18-oz.) can (2¼ c.) unsweetened pineapple juice
Cinnamon sticks for each cup

(continued)

In a large saucepan heat first 2 ingredients until boils. Reduce heat, cover and simmer for 5 minutes. Stir in remaining ingredients except cinnamon sticks and simmer for 5 minutes longer.

Joan Johnson

WINE COOLER

1 c. cranberry juice cocktail
1 c. Sprite

1 c. orange juice
1 c. white wine

Mix all together and add orange and lime slices on top. This is a nice refreshing drink without wine if preferred.

Patsy Pomeroy

Recipe Favorites

Soups & Salads

Helpful Hints

- If the soup is not intended as the main course, count on 1 quart to serve 6. As the main dish, plan on 1 quart to serve 2.
- After cooking vegetables, pour any water and leftover vegetable pieces into a freezer container. When full, add tomato juice and seasoning to create a money-saving "free soup."
- Instant potatoes help thicken soups and stews.
- A leaf of lettuce dropped in a pot of soup absorbs grease from the top – remove the lettuce and serve. You can also make soup the day before, chill, and scrape off the hardened fat that rises to the top.
- To cut down on odors when cooking cabbage or cauliflower, add a little vinegar to the water and don't overcook.
- Three large stalks of celery, chopped and added to about two cups of beans (navy, brown, pinto, etc.), make the dish easier to digest.
- Fresh is best, but to reduce time in the kitchen, use canned or frozen broths or bouillon bases. Canned or frozen vegetables, such as peas, green beans, and corn, also work well.
- Ideally, cold soups should be served in chilled bowls.
- Perk up soggy lettuce by spritzing it with a mixture of lemon juice and cold water.
- You can easily remove egg shells from hard-boiled eggs if you quickly rinse the eggs in cold water after they are boiled. Add a drop of food coloring to help distinguish cooked eggs from raw ones.
- Your fruit salads will look better when you use an egg slicer to make perfect slices of strawberries, kiwis, or bananas.
- The ratio for a vinaigrette is typically 3 parts oil to 1 part vinegar.
- For salads, cook pasta al dente (slightly chewy to the bite). This allows the pasta to absorb some of the dressing and not become mushy.
- Fresh vegetables require little seasoning or cooking. If the vegetable is old, dress it up with sauces or seasoning.
- Chill the serving plates to keep the salad crisp.
- Fruit juices, such as pineapple and orange, can be used as salad dressing by adding a little olive oil, nutmeg, and honey.

Copyright © Morris Press Cookbooks

Soups & Salads

JOAN'S CHICKEN SOUP

3 med. chicken breasts
1 can cream of chicken soup
1 (16-oz.) can vegetables, drained
3 c. sm. diced potatoes
Italian noodles
2 tsp. chicken bouillon

Boil 3 medium chicken breasts. Let cool and cut up in strips or cubes. Add 2 heaping teaspoons chicken bouillon, 1 can cream of chicken soup, 3 cups small diced potatoes and 1 (16-ounce) can drained vegetables. Cook until potatoes are slightly done; add Italian noodles and chicken chunks. Cook slightly longer adding salt and pepper to taste.

Joan Johnson

CLASSIC ONION SOUP

4 c. thinly sliced onions
1 clove garlic, finely chopped
1/4 c. butter
5 1/2 c. water
1/2 c. dry white wine (opt.)
8 tsp. Wyler's beef-flavored instant bouillon
6 slices French bread, 1/4-inch thick, buttered & toasted
6 slices natural Swiss cheese, cut in half crosswise

In a large saucepan cook onion and garlic in butter until onions are golden brown. Add water, wine (if desired) and bouillon; bring to a boil. Reduce heat and simmer for 30 minutes to blend flavors. Place soup in 6 oven-proof soup bowls. Top each serving with a bread slice and cheese. Broil until cheese melts. Serve immediately.

Patsy Pomeroy

POTATO AND GROUND BEEF SOUP

1 lb. ground beef
4 c. cubed, peeled potatoes
1 sm. onion, chopped
3 (8-oz.) cans tomato sauce
4 c. water
2 tsp. salt
1 1/2 tsp. pepper
1/2-1 tsp. hot pepper sauce

(continued)

In a Dutch oven or large pot brown ground beef. Drain and add potatoes, onion and tomato sauce. Stir in water, salt, pepper and hot pepper sauce; bring to a boil. Reduce heat and simmer for 1 hour or until potatoes are tender and soup is thickened.

Joan Johnson

JOAN'S CREAMY POTATO SOUP

6 med. potatoes
1 sm. onion
2-3 T. flour
2 slices cheese

Salt and pepper
$1/2$ c. sm. pieces chopped ham
1-2 c. milk

Peel and cube about 6 medium potatoes and cover with water in large pot and cut up a small onion into the water. Cook until potatoes are tender and add 2-3 heaping tablespoons flour with 1 cup water; add to potato mixture. Then add salt and pepper and 2 slices of cheese. Stir in 1-2 cups milk. Mash potatoes while still on medium heat, stirring constantly. Add about $1/2$ cup small pieces of ham and top with grated cheese.

Joan Johnson

CHEESY WILD RICE SOUP

1 (6-oz.) pkg. quick cooking long-grain & wild rice mix
4 c. milk
1 (8-oz.) pkg. Velveeta cheese, cubed

1 can cream of potato soup, condensed
$1/2$ lb. bacon, cooked & crumbled

Cook rice according to directions on package. When rice is done stir in milk, soup and cheese; mix well and stir until cheese is melted. Garnish with bacon. Serves 6 to 8.

Patsy Pomeroy

SHRIMP OR LOBSTER BISQUE

1 stick butter
½ c. flour
1 qt. half & half
1 c. milk
2 c. or 2 sm. cans tomato juice
2 c. lobster or shrimp, cut into small pieces
1 dash cayenne pepper
1 T. Old Bay seafood seasoning
Salt and white pepper to taste
1 egg

Melt butter in large pot gradually add half & half and stir until thickened. Add milk and tomato juice stirring. Beat egg and add slowly stirring constantly. Add cayenne pepper, seafood seasoning, salt and pepper. Mix thoroughly. Add lobster or shrimp and continue stirring until well blended. Simmer.

Tip: If desired you can add a dash of sherry to bisque.

Connie Cullers

CREAM OF SPINACH SOUP

1 (10-oz.) pkg. frozen chopped spinach, thawed
½ c. chopped onion
2 T. butter, melted
3 T. all-purpose flour
1 qt. milk
⅛ tsp. pepper

Drain spinach thoroughly; set aside. Sauté onion in butter in a large saucepan until tender. Add flour, stirring until smooth. Cook for 1 minute stirring constantly. Gradually add milk, stir in spinach, salt and pepper. Cook over medium heat stirring constantly until mixture is thickened and bubbly. Makes 1 quart.

Patsy Pomeroy

LEFTOVER THANKSGIVING TURKEY SOUP

In a large soup pot cover turkey carcass with water and boil for a few minutes then reduce heat and simmer until meat falls off bone. With slotted ladle scoop out turkey bones and skin and throw out. Check carefully for small bones in pot of turkey meat and broth. Salt and pepper to taste. Add any leftover giblet gravy or turkey broth left from Thanksgiving. Add noodles (I prefer dumpling noodles) and cook

(continued)

until tender. Noodles will help thicken soup. It is delicious served over leftover dressing.

Patsy Pomeroy

AMBROSIA MOLD

1 (8-oz.) can crushed pineapple with juice
2 c. boiling water
1 can mandarin orange segments, drained
1 (8-serving) pkg. Jello brand orange-flavored gelatin

1½ c. miniature marshmallows
½ c. coconut (opt.)
1¾ c. Cool Whip whipped topping, thawed

Drain pineapple, reserving liquid. Add cold water to liquid to measure 1 cup. Stir boiling water into gelatin in large bowl for 2 minutes or until completely dissolved. Stir in measured liquid. Refrigerate for 1¼ hours or until slightly thickened (consistency of unbeaten egg whites). Stir in whipped topping with wire whisk until smooth. Refrigerate for 10 minutes or until mixture will mound. Stir in oranges and pineapple, marshmallows and coconut. Spoon into 6-cup mold. Refrigerate for 4 hours or until firm. Unmold. Makes 10 servings.

Joan Johnson

MARINATED BROCCOLI SALAD

2 lg. bunches broccoli
¼ c. red onion
1 c. raisins

½ c. sugar
1 T. apple cider vinegar
Bacon

Mix together and marinate in refrigerator for 24 hours. When serving crumble the bacon over it.

Joan Johnson

MARINATED COLESLAW

1 onion, chopped
1 T. sugar
1 c. vinegar
1 tsp. dry mustard
2 tsp. celery seed

2 tsp. salt
1 c. salad oil
Cabbage
¾ c. sugar

(continued)

Combine 1 chopped red onion, 1 tablespoon sugar, 1 cup vinegar, 2 teaspoons salt, 2 teaspoons celery seed and 1 teaspoon dry mustard. Bring to a boil then add 1 cup salad oil and heat but do not boil. Chop up cabbage and add ¾ cup sugar to it. Pour hot mixture over cabbage. Marinate in refrigerator for at least 24 hours.

Joan Johnson

CUCUMBER SALAD

1-2 cucumbers, sliced
Salt and pepper
10 oz. sour cream
1 T. vinegar

Tabasco sauce
2 T. chopped chives
1 tsp. dill seed

Salt the cucumbers and let stand for 30 minutes. Drain the water off and mix cucumbers with 10 ounces of sour cream, 1 tablespoon vinegar, 1 or 2 drops of Tabasco sauce, 2 tablespoons chopped chives, 1 teaspoon dill seed, salt and pepper. Let sit in refrigerator for a couple of hours.

Joan Johnson

JOAN'S CHUNKY FRUIT CHICKEN SALAD

Raisins
Celery
Poppy seed dressing

Sliced & seeded red grapes
Chunks of chicken
Chopped apple

Boil white pieces of chicken and then cut into chunks to make about 2 cups. Add to this chopped apple, sliced and seeded red grapes, celery and raisins. Pour poppy seed dressing over the salad and stir. Refrigerate and add chopped walnuts.

Joan Johnson

FROZEN CRANBERRY BANANA SALAD

1 (20-oz.) can pineapple tidbits
5 med. firm bananas, halved lengthwise & sliced
½ c. sugar
1 (12-oz.) ctn. frozen whipped topping, thawed

1 (16-oz.) can whole cranberry sauce
½ c. chopped walnuts

(continued)

Drain pineapple juice into a medium bowl; set pineapple aside. Add bananas to the juice. In a large bowl combine cranberry sauce and sugar. Remove bananas, discarding the juice and add to cranberry mixture. Stir in pineapple, whipped topping and nuts. Pour into a 9 x 13 x 2-inch dish. Freeze until solid. Remove from freezer 15 minutes before cutting.

Joan Johnson

Fruit Salad

3 lg. cans chunk pineapple
3 sm. cans mandarin oranges
1 lb. seedless grapes
1 bottle maraschino cherries
1 lg. box vanilla pudding (not instant)
8 oz. pecans
6-8 bananas, sliced

Combine drained pineapple, oranges and cherries. Make pudding as directed on package. Let cool. Pour over fruit and let stand overnight. Stir next morning and add pecans, sliced bananas and grapes before serving. Makes enough salad for 10 people.

Patsy Pomeroy

Frozen Fruit Salad

2 c. sour cream
2 T. lemon juice
1 c. sugar
1/8 tsp. salt
1 (8-oz.) can crushed pineapple, drained
2 bananas, diced
1/4 c. pecans, chopped
1 lg. jar maraschino cherries, chopped (use some juice for color & flavor)

Mix all ingredients together in a large bowl. Place in 9 x 13-inch pan or in paper cupcake liners set in muffin tins. Freeze overnight. Remove from freezer about 15 minutes before serving. Serves 12.

Patsy Pomeroy

Congealed Strawberry Salad

1 (family-size) or 2 sm. pkgs. strawberry gelatin
1½ c. boiling water
1 lg. pkg. frozen strawberries, partially thawed
1 can crushed pineapple, undrained
2-3 bananas, sliced
1 c. chopped pecans
1 c. sour cream

Dissolve gelatin in boiling water. Cool slightly. Add strawberries, pecans and bananas. Pour half the mixture into a 8 x 12 x 2-inch glass dish and chill until set. Keep other half at room temperature for time being. When set spread sour cream over top and pour and spread remainder of mixture over this. Chill until firm.

Joan Johnson

Strawberry Jello Salad

2 sm. pkgs. strawberry Jello
2 (10-oz.) pkgs. frozen strawberries, thawed
2 med. bananas, mashed
1 pt. sour cream
1 c. boiling water
1 (14-oz.) can crushed pineapple, drained
1 c. pecans, chopped

Combine Jello with water. Mix well. Fold in all at once strawberries with juice, drained pineapple, bananas and nuts. Turn ½ of mixture into 12 x 18 x 2-inch casserole. Chill until firm (about 1½ hours). Evenly spread top with sour cream. Gently smooth rest of Jello mixture over top and chill until firm. Cut into squares and serve on top of lettuce. Serves 8.

Patsy Pomeroy

Strawberry Pretzel Salad

Crust:

3 c. pretzels
1 c. butter, melted
¼ c. sugar

Crush pretzels and blend in sugar and melted butter. Press into the bottom of a 9 x 13-inch glass dish. Bake at 350° for 10 minutes.

Next Layer:

1 (8-oz.) pkg. cream cheese
1 c. sugar
2 c. Cool Whip or real whipped cream

(continued)

Combine ingredients and smooth over cooled pretzel crust.

Third Layer:

1 (6-oz.) pkg. strawberry instant Jello
2 c. water
1 pt. frozen strawberries

Bring water to a boil and mix in instant Jello. Stir in frozen strawberries. Set up in refrigerator until slightly firm then spread over cream cheese layer. Cover and refrigerate overnight. Put remaining Cool Whip on top of Jello before you serve.

Patsy Pomeroy

WEST INDIES SALAD

1 lb. white crab meat
1 lg. onion, diced

Place ½ pound crab meat in medium-size bowl; cover with ½ of the onions. Repeat with the remainder of the crab meat and then the onions.

Dressing:

4 oz. water
4 oz. Wesson oil
3 oz. white distilled vinegar

Pour the liquids over crab meat and onions. Salt and pepper as desired. Cover; place in refrigerator for 12 hours. Mix well before serving.

Joan Johnson

1905 SALAD

1 head iceberg lettuce
4 tomatoes, diced
6 oz. Swiss cheese, shredded
6 oz. smoked ham, julienne
½ c. Spanish olives
4 T. Romano cheese

Dressing:

8 cloves garlic, minced
2 tsp. oregano
2 T. Worcestershire sauce
1 lemon, juiced
1 c. virgin olive oil
½ c. white vinegar
Salt and pepper to taste

(continued)

Mix all ingredients together and top with dressing. The better the cheese the better the salad.

Tip: You can substitute Parmesan for Romano cheese. You can use sliced olives instead of whole. Do not mix the salad ingredients until ready to serve or the lettuce will wilt. The dressing can be made in advance.

Patsy Pomeroy

Recipe Favorites

Recipe Favorites

Vegetables & Side Dishes

Helpful Hints

- When preparing a casserole, make an additional batch to freeze for when you're short on time. Use within 2 months.

- To keep hot oil from splattering, sprinkle a little salt or flour in the pan before frying.

- To prevent pasta from boiling over, place a wooden spoon or fork across the top of the pot while the pasta is boiling.

- Boil all vegetables that grow above ground without a cover.

- Never soak vegetables after slicing; they will lose much of their nutritional value.

- Green pepper may change the flavor of frozen casseroles. Clove, garlic, and pepper flavors get stronger when frozen, while sage, onion, and salt become more mild.

- For an easy no-mess side dish, grill vegetables along with your meat.

- Store dried pasta, rice (except brown rice), and whole grains in tightly covered containers in a cool, dry place. Refrigerate brown rice and freeze grains if you will not use them within 5 months.

- A few drops of lemon juice added to simmering rice will keep the grains separated.

- When cooking greens, add a teaspoon of sugar to the water to help vegetables retain their fresh colors.

- To dress up buttered, cooked vegetables, sprinkle them with toasted sesame seeds, toasted chopped nuts, canned french-fried onions, grated cheese, or slightly crushed seasoned croutons.

- Soufflé dishes are designed with straight sides to help your soufflé rise. Ramekins work well for single-serve casseroles.

- A little vinegar or lemon juice added to potatoes before draining will make them extra white when mashed.

- To avoid toughened beans or corn, add salt midway through cooking.

- If your pasta sauce seems a little dry, add a few tablespoons of the pasta's cooking water.

- To prevent cheese from sticking to a grater, spray the grater with cooking spray before beginning.

Copyright © Morris Press Cookbooks

Vegetables & Side Dishes

Buttery Cinnamon Skillet Apples

1/3 butter
1/2-3/4 c. sugar
2 T. cornstarch
1 1/2 c. water

1/4-1/2 tsp. cinnamon
4 med. cooking apples, cored, unpeeled & cut in half

In a skillet melt butter over medium heat. Stir in sugar and cornstarch; mix well. Add remaining ingredients. Cover; cook over medium heat spooning sauce over apples occasionally until apples are fork tender and sauce is thickened. To serve, place 2 apple halves in individual dessert dish; spoon 1/2 cup sauce over each.

Joan Johnson

Cabbage Casserole

1 med. cabbage
1 can tomato soup
1 can water
1 lb. browned ground beef

1/2 c. chopped onion
1/3 c. green pepper
1/2 c. uncooked rice
1 c. cheddar cheese

Cook onion and pepper in skillet, add ground beef, salt and pepper. Add rice to meat mixture. Place chopped cabbage in long casserole dish. Pour meat mixture evenly over cabbage. Add tomato soup and water. Cover with foil and bake for 1 hour at 350° then top with cheese.

Joan Johnson

Marinated Carrots

2 lbs. carrots

Slice on a slant, cook until tender and drain. Mix together:

(continued)

1 lg. onion, sliced
1 green pepper, chopped
1 can tomato soup
1 c. sugar
½ c. oil

½ dry mustard
¾ c. cider vinegar
1 tsp. salt
¼ tsp. pepper

Add mixture to carrots in casserole dish. Refrigerate overnight.

Connie Cullers

Pickled Carrot Dish

2 lbs. carrots
1 can tomato soup
¾ c. white vinegar
½ c. Wesson oil
1 tsp. Worcestershire sauce

⅛ tsp. pepper
1 tsp. prepared mustard
1 med. onion, sliced
1 c. sugar
1 tsp. salt

Scrape and cut carrots ¼ inch thick. Cook carrots until tender. Drain and add onions. Mix remaining ingredients and pour over carrots. Place into large bowl with lid sealed tight. Let marinate in refrigerator overnight.

Joan Johnson

Cauliflower Casserole

Cook 1 head cauliflower; drain and place in baking dish. Top heavily with cheddar cheese then add white sauce.

White Sauce:

2 T. butter
2 T. flour

¼ tsp. salt
1 c. milk

Cook until thick. Pour over cauliflower and cheese then top with more cheddar cheese. Bake at 350° for 20 minutes.

Joan Johnson

Fresh Collard Greens

1 bunch fresh collard greens   4 strips bacon

Wash collards several times in sink to make sure all gritty sand is removed. In a large pot fry bacon until crisp. Remove bacon and leave

(continued)

grease in pot. Place clean collards in pot and sauté on low heat stirring regularly until wilted. Add water to cover and add crumbled bacon. Cook on medium heat for about 1½ hours until tender. Add water as needed.

Patsy Pomeroy

GARLIC GRITS

1 c. grits
2 sticks butter
½ c. milk
8 oz. garlic cheese
2 eggs, beaten

Cook grits according to directions. Melt cheese and butter. Add eggs and milk to cheese mixture. Fold all into grits. Bake in 9 x 13-inch dish at 350° for 30 minutes. Serves 4-6.

Patsy Pomeroy

MACARONI AND CHEESE

½ box elbow macaroni, cooked according to box directions
½ stick butter
1 lg. block Kraft sharp cheddar cheese
1 c. milk
1 egg, slightly beaten

Place cooked macaroni in baking dish. Mix in butter until melted. Blend together with wire whisk milk and egg. Pour over macaroni noodles. Slice block of cheese into square pieces to cover top of macaroni. Bake at 350° for about 30 minutes or until cheese is melted and milk and egg have set.

Patsy Pomeroy

FRIED OKRA

1 lb. fresh okra
½ c. cornmeal
1 c. vegetable oil
Salt and pepper to taste

Wash and cut okra into small disc. Salt and pepper. Dredge in cornmeal until well coated. Fry in hot oil until nice and crispy. Drain on plate with paper towel.

Patsy Pomeroy

VIDALIA ONION PIE

1 (9-inch) pie crust
4 Vidalia onions, halved & sliced
2 T. butter
1 c. grated cheddar cheese
3 eggs

1 c. half & half cream
1 tsp. Coleman's mustard
Little cayenne pepper
Pinch of salt

Prebake pie crust for about 15 minutes. Sauté onions in butter. Put in pre-baked pie crust. Mix eggs, half & half, mustard and seasonings. Pour over onions. Sprinkle with cheese. Bake at 350° for about 40 minutes.

Patsy Pomeroy

PINEAPPLE BREAD CASSEROLE

4 eggs, slightly beaten
3/4 c. sugar
1/4 c. butter, melted

4 slices white bread, cubed
2 T. flour
1 can crushed pineapple with juice

Combine eggs, sugar, butter, flour and pineapple. Mix in bread. Pour into a greased 1½-quart casserole dish. Bake for 1 hour at 350°.

Tip: You may use whole-wheat bread if desired.

Patsy Pomeroy

AU GRATIN POTATOES

8 med. potatoes
6 T. flour
1 lg. onion, chopped
½ green pepper, chopped
Paprika
Salt and pepper to taste

6 T. butter
1½ c. grated sharp cheese
2 T. fresh parsley
3 c. milk
Thin sliced cheese

Cook peeled potatoes, onions and peppers together until done. Make sauce using butter, flour, milk and grated cheese, salt and pepper. Add this to potatoes along with parsley and mix well. Transfer to baking dish, cover with more thin sliced cheddar cheese, sprinkle with paprika and bake in 300° oven for 30 minutes.

Joan Johnson

CRAB STUFFED POTATOES

5 med. Idaho potatoes
1 c. fresh crab meat or 6½ oz. canned crab or imitation crab
8 oz. butter
½ c. light cream
1 tsp. salt
4 tsp. grated onion
2 c. grated cheddar cheese
½ tsp. paprika
¼ tsp. white pepper

Bake potatoes until tender. Cut lengthwise and scoop out pulp. Whip together potatoes, butter, cream, salt, pepper, onion and cheese. Add a little more cream if necessary. With a fork mix in crab meat and refill four halved shells. (The extra potato is to ensure plenty of stuffing.) Sprinkle with paprika and reheat in a 400° oven for about 15 minutes. Serves 8. Can be made ahead of time. Freezes well.

Patsy Pomeroy

MAKE AHEAD CHEESY MASHED POTATOES

Cook and mash 8 potatoes. Add:

1 stick butter
8 oz. sour cream
2 green onions & tops, chopped
Salt and pepper to taste
Shredded cheddar cheese

Mix together and put in a casserole dish. Top with cheddar cheese. Bake at 350° for 20 minutes.

Connie Cullers

CHEESY POTATOES

1 (2-lb.) pkg. frozen hash brown potatoes, partially thawed
1 (16-oz.) ctn. sour cream
2 c. mild cheddar cheese
1 c. shredded Monterey Jack cheese
½ c. onion
½ c. chopped green & red bell peppers
1 T. chicken bouillon granules
½ c. chopped green & red bell peppers (opt.)

Grease a 9 x 13-inch dish. Combine potatoes, sour cream, 1½ cups cheddar cheese and remaining ingredients. Mix well. Place in the baking dish. Bake for 55-60 minutes. Top with remaining cheese and bake for 3-5 minutes longer.

Joan Johnson

GREEN PEPPER POTATOES

6 med. potatoes
1 med. onion
½ green pepper

1 stick margarine
Salt and pepper to taste

Peel and slice potatoes to make round slices. Slice onion in round slices. Slice pepper in strips. Place these ingredients onto a long strip of foil. Cut up margarine over top, salt and pepper. Twist each end of foil then place on BBQ grill and cook along with the steaks.

Joan Johnson

POTATO CASSEROLE

24 oz. or larger bag frozen hash browns
1 tsp. salt
1 (16-oz.) ctn. sour cream
2 cans cream of chicken soup or soup like it

1 stick butter or margarine
½ c. chopped onion
¼ tsp. pepper
1¾ c. shredded cheese

Mix sour cream, soup, melted butter, onion, salt and pepper; fold in cheese. Break apart hash browns and add to mix. Bake in 9 x 13 x 2-inch pan at 350° for 30 minutes. Top with 2 cups crushed cornflakes (etc.) and 1 stick melted butter. Bake for 15 minutes or more. May want to use 2 cans soup for a whole batch and 1 can for ½ batch.

Patsy Pomeroy

SOUTHERN MASHED POTATOES

3 lg. Idaho potatoes
¾ stick butter

¼ c. milk or cream
1 tsp. salt

Peel and chop potatoes. Boil in water until tender. Drain well and place in mixing bowl. While hot add butter in chunks and mix well until butter is dissolved. Add salt. Using a hand mixer beat until all blended together. Add milk to mixture slowly until nice and smooth. Do not overmix.

Patsy Pomeroy

Rice Casserole

1 c. rice
1 can chicken broth
1 can mushrooms & juice
1 sm. onion, chopped
½ stick butter

Mix all ingredients together; cover and cook at 350° for 45 minutes. Serves 8.

Connie Cullers

Mother's Squash Casserole

Cook 2 pounds squash with onions and seasoning until tender. Spoon into baking dish and add:

1 pkg. dry cream of chicken soup
1 egg, beaten
½ stick margarine
1 c. grated cheddar cheese

Mix well, then top with Ritz cracker crumbs. Bake at 350° for 35 to 45 minutes.

Joan Johnson

Cooked Squash and Tomatoes

Several fresh squash, cut up
1 zucchini, chopped
1 fresh tomato, chopped
A little green pepper, chopped (opt.)
½ onion, chopped

Melt ¾ stick of butter in skillet. Add vegetables and simmer on low for 15 to 20 minutes. There is usually enough juice from tomatoes but a little water can be added if needed.

Patsy Pomeroy

Squash Casserole

1 stick butter
1 pkg. herbal Pepperidge Farm stuffing
2 lbs. cooked squash & onions
1 (8-oz.) pkg. cream cheese
1 can cream of chicken soup
1 (8-oz.) pkg. shredded cheddar cheese

Mix ½ of package of Pepperidge Farm stuffing with ½ stick butter, then press down into a baking dish. Mix stewed squash with cream

(continued)

of chicken soup, sour cream, remaining herbal stuffing. Spoon into baking dish. Top with shredded cheddar cheese. Bake at 350° for 45 minutes.

Joan Johnson

Sweet Potato and Apple Casserole

3 med. sweet potatoes
½ c. firmly packed brown sugar
1 tsp. ground cinnamon
1 tsp. ground nutmeg
2 lg. cooking apples, peeled & cut into ¼-inch rings
Streusel Topping

Cook unpeeled sweet potatoes in water until tender. Drain, cool and slice into ¼-inch rounds. Combine brown sugar, cinnamon and nutmeg. Layer sweet potatoes, apples and brown sugar mixture in a lightly greased 11 x 7 x 1½-inch baking dish beginning and ending with sweet potatoes. Bake at 350°. Sprinkle with Streusel Topping.

Streusel Topping:

¼ c. all-purpose flour
¼ c. packed brown sugar
¼ c. butter or margarine
¼ c. chopped pecans

Combine all ingredients together then add to top of potatoes.

Joan Johnson

Sweet Potato Casserole

1½ lbs. sweet potatoes
½ c. granulated sugar
½ c. milk
1 egg, beaten
3 T. butter, cubed
1 tsp. vanilla
½ c. packed brown sugar
⅓ c. all-purpose flour
2 T. butter
½ c. pecan pieces
Pecan halves (opt.)

Scrub and peel sweet potatoes. Cut off and discard woody portions and ends. Cut potatoes into cubes. Cook covered in a small amount of boiling water for 25 to 35 minutes or until tender. Drain. Combine hot sweet potatoes, granulated sugar, milk, egg, 3 tablespoons butter and vanilla. With a wooden spoon stir to break up potatoes but not completely mash them. Put mixture into a greased 2-quart square baking dish. Combine brown sugar and flour; cut in the 2 tablespoons butter until mixture resembles coarse crumbs. Stir in pecan pieces and sprinkle crumb mixture on top of potatoes. Bake uncovered in a 350°

(continued)

oven for about 25 minutes or until set. Garnish with pecan halves, if desired. Makes 8 side dish servings.

Patsy Pomeroy

Fried Green Tomatoes

2-3 lg. green tomatoes
1 lb. bacon, fried crisp & crumbled into bits & save grease

All-purpose white flour
Salt to taste
8 oz. mozzarella cheese

Slice tomatoes in circles about a centimeter thick. Sprinkle with salt. Dredge in flour. Using the same pan and grease from bacon drippings fry the tomatoes until they are a light golden brown. Place on plate and shred mozzarella cheese on top while still hot. Immediately crumble the bacon on top of the cheese.

Patsy Pomeroy

Tomato Pie

1 (9-inch) refrigerated pie crust
2 ripe tomatoes, sliced
3/4 lb. grated Monterey Jack cheese
1 tsp. dried basil
1 tsp. oregano

1/2 tsp. salt
1/8 tsp. pepper
2 green onions, thinly sliced
2 T. fresh bread crumbs
2 T. butter, melted

Preheat oven to 425°. Fit pie crust into 9-inch glass pie plate. Crimp the edges and prick all over with a fork. Bake for 12 to 15 minutes until lightly brown. Let cool on wire rack. Sprinkle the cheese evenly over the crust. Top with overlapping tomato slices to cover pie crust. Sprinkle spices evenly over tomatoes. Spread onion on top. Sprinkle with bread crumbs and drizzle the butter on top. Bake for 20 minutes. Allow to sit for at least 10 minutes before cutting into wedges.

Patsy Pomeroy

Yorkshire Pudding

1 c. sifted flour
2 eggs
1/2 tsp. salt

1 c. milk
1/4 c. hot beef drippings

Mix 1 cup sifted flour and 1/2 teaspoon salt gradually stirring in 2 eggs, well beaten. Add 1 cup milk and beat with rotary beater until

(continued)

smooth. Pour into hot shallow pan containing ¼ cup hot beef drippings and bake at 400° for 25-30 minutes.

Connie Cullers

Recipe Favorites

Main Dishes

Helpful Hints

- Certain meats, like ribs and pot roast, can be parboiled before grilling to reduce the fat content.

- Pound meat lightly with a mallet or rolling pin, pierce with a fork, sprinkle lightly with meat tenderizer, and add marinade. Refrigerate for 20 minutes and cook or grill for a quick and succulent meat.

- Marinating is a cinch if you use a plastic bag. The meat stays in the marinade and it's easy to turn. Cleanup is easy; just toss the bag.

- It's easier to thinly slice meat if it's partially frozen.

- Adding tomatoes to roasts naturally tenderizes the meat as tomatoes contain an acid that works well to break down meats.

- Whenever possible, cut meat across the grain; this will make it easier to eat and also give it a more attractive appearance.

- When frying meat, sprinkle paprika on the meat to turn it golden brown.

- Thaw all meats in the refrigerator for maximum safety.

- Refrigerate poultry promptly after purchasing. Keep it in the coldest part of your refrigerator for up to 2 days. Freeze poultry for longer storage. Never leave poultry at room temperature for over 2 hours.

- When frying chicken, canola oil provides a milder taste, and it contains healthier amounts of saturated and polyunsaturated fats. Do not cover the chicken once it has finished cooking because covering will cause the coating to lose its crispness.

- One pound of boneless chicken equals approximately 3 cups of cubed chicken.

- Generally, red meats should reach 160° and poultry should reach 180° before serving. If preparing fish, the surface of the fish should flake off with a fork.

- Rub lemon juice on fish before cooking to enhance the flavor and help maintain a good color.

- Scaling a fish is easier if vinegar is rubbed on the scales first.

- When grilling fish, the rule of thumb is to cook 5 minutes on each side per inch of thickness. For example, cook a 2-inch thick fillet for 10 minutes per side. Before grilling, rub with oil to seal in moisture.

Copyright © Morris Press Cookbooks

Main Dishes

ITALIAN BEEF 'N CHEESE DINNER

1 lb. ground beef, cooked
1 (6-oz.) can tomato paste
1 tsp. oregano
½ c. chopped olives (opt.)
¼ c. chopped onion
1 tsp. salt
¼ tsp. garlic powder
1 (4-oz.) can mushrooms, undrained
1½ c. mozzarella, cheddar or American cheese

Combine all ingredients except cheese. Mix thoroughly. Spoon into Krazy Crust. Bake for 18 to 28 minutes until crust is golden brown. Sprinkle with cheese; return to oven to melt cheese. Add tomato and shredded lettuce if desired.

Krazy Crust:

½ c. all-purpose flour
½ tsp. salt
½ tsp. baking powder
¼ c. Crisco shortening
½ c. sour cream
1 egg

Combine all ingredients in a medium bowl. Stir until blended. Batter will be lumpy. Lightly grease and flour bottom and sides of 9-inch metal or 10-inch glass pie pan. Spread batter evenly over bottom and sides. Bake at 425°.

Joan Johnson

MAKE AHEAD BREAKFAST CASSEROLE

1 pkg. sausage, cooked, drained
4 c. cubed day old bread
10 eggs, slightly beaten
4 c. milk
2 c. sharp cheddar cheese
½ c. peeled, chopped tomatoes (opt.)
½ c. mushrooms (opt.)
1 tsp. salt
1 tsp. dry mustard
¼ tsp. onion powder
Pepper to taste

Place bread in well greased baking dish topped with cooked sausage. Sprinkle with cheese. Combine eggs, milk, mustard, salt, pepper and onion powder. Pour evenly over top. Cover and chill overnight. Bake

(continued)

uncovered for 1 hour at 325°. Tent with foil if top begins to brown too quickly.

Connie Cullers

CAROL'S CASSEROLE

1 lb. hamburger meat
Salt and pepper
1 sm. jar mushrooms, sliced
1 green pepper, chopped
¼ c. green olives, sliced

½ onion, chopped
1 (8-oz.) can tomato sauce
1 sm. can tomato paste
Egg noodles, cooked, drained
Grated cheddar cheese

Cook hamburger meat, salt and pepper to taste. Add onion, mushrooms and green pepper. Add sliced olives, tomato sauce and tomato paste. Simmer for 15 minutes. Put in 9 x 13-inch baking dish with noodles. Spread grated cheese on top. Bake at 350° until cheese is melted. Serves 4.

Patsy Pomeroy

BROCCOLI-CHICKEN CASSEROLE

1 fryer chicken, cooked & deboned
1 pkg. frozen broccoli spears, cooked & drained
1 can cream of chicken soup, undiluted
½ c. mayonnaise

½ tsp. lemon juice
½ c. bread crumbs
2 T. butter or margarine, melted
1 pkg. sliced almonds
½ c. shredded cheddar cheese

Combine soup, mayonnaise and lemon juice; stir well. Set aside. Arrange broccoli in lightly greased 9 x 13-inch pan. Top with chicken and soup mixture. Combine bread crumbs and butter stirring well. Sprinkle over top of casserole. Bake at 350° for 30 minutes; remove and sprinkle cheese over top; return to oven for 5 minutes or until cheese is melted.

Patsy Pomeroy

CHICKEN CASSEROLE

4 boneless chicken breasts, cooked & cubed
1 can cream of mushroom soup
8 oz. sour cream

1 c. grated cheddar cheese
½ stick butter
Ritz crackers

(continued)

Place chicken in casserole dish and pour soup, sour cream and cheddar cheese in. Crumble Ritz crackers and melt butter on top of chicken mixture. Bake at 350° for 25 minutes.

Connie Cullers

CHICKEN WRAPPED IN BACON

6 boneless, skinless chicken
  breasts
1 can cream of mushroom soup
1 pt. sour cream
Cheddar cheese
1 sm. can mushrooms
6 slices bacon

Flatten chicken breasts. Cut cheese in long chunks and wrap each breast in the cheese and bacon. Lay inside the casserole dish while mixing the sour cream, cream of mushroom soup and mushrooms together. Pour over chicken and bake uncovered in 275° oven for approximately 3 hours.

Connie Cullers

CHICKEN PARMESAN

4 boneless, skinless chicken breast
  halves
1 egg, slightly beaten
1¾ c. Prego spaghetti sauce
2 T. butter
½ c. seasoned bread crumbs
½ c. shredded mozzarella cheese
¼ c. chopped fresh parsley
1 T. grated Parmesan cheese

Flatten chicken to even thickness. Dip chicken into egg, then crumbs to coat. In a skillet over medium heat brown chicken on both sides with butter. Add Prego sauce and reduce heat. Cover; simmer for 10 minutes. Sprinkle with cheeses and parsley. Cover; simmer for 5 minutes or until cheese melts.

Joan Johnson

CONNIE'S CHICKEN CASSEROLE

Cook 4 chicken breasts in water. Add 1 tablespoon butter, salt and pepper to taste. Cook and drain 2 packages chopped broccoli. Add 2 cans of cream of mushroom soup, 1 jar of Cheez Whiz and 2 cups of cooked rice. Cut up chicken and add to mixture. Add a little of broth.

(continued)

Put in casserole dish and top with cracker crumbs mixed with melted butter. Sprinkle grated cheese on top. Bake for 30 minutes at 400°.

Connie Cullers

STEWED CHICKEN

1 whole chicken, cut up

Wash chicken and dry. Coat chicken lightly in flour. Heat enough oil in medium, heavy saucepan to just cover the bottom. Place floured chicken in oil and slowly brown. Remove chicken, add enough flour (3 to 4 tablespoons) to oil in pan for gravy. Stir well until lightly browned, then add water to mixture to make a gravy. Add salt and pepper. Cut up 1 stalk of celery, add to gravy; add the chicken back into the gravy and allow to smother for about 20 minutes. Serve over rice.

Joan Johnson

CHICKEN AND RICE CASSEROLE

2 c. cooked rice
3 c. cooked, diced chicken
1 sm. onion
2 cans cream of mushroom soup
2 T. lemon juice
$1/4$ c. celery
4 boiled eggs, chopped
1 c. mayonnaise
1 tsp. salt
3 oz. slivered almonds

Mix all ingredients together. Put in 9 x 12-inch casserole. Melt 4 tablespoons butter, mix 1 cup bread crumbs and brown, Put in top of casserole. Bake at 350° for 30-40 minutes covered.

Connie Cullers

CHICKEN POT PIE

3 c. cooked, cubed chicken
3 hard-boiled eggs (opt.)
1 can cream of celery soup
1 can cream of chicken soup
$1^{1}/_{2}$ c. chicken broth
2 T. cornstarch
1 (16-oz.) pkg. frozen mixed
   vegetables, thawed & drained
1 c. self-rising flour
1 c. milk
1 stick butter or margarine,
   melted

Preheat oven to 350°. Place chicken in bottom of 9 x 13-inch dish. Slice eggs placing on top of chicken. Add mixed vegetables. Mix soups

(continued)

and cornstarch; pour over vegetables. Mix butter, flour and milk; pour over all. Bake for 1 hour.

Patsy Pomeroy

ONE DISH CHICKEN & RICE BAKE

1 can cream of chicken soup
1 c. water
¼ tsp. paprika
¼ tsp. pepper
4 skinless, boneless chicken breast halves
¾ c. uncooked long-grain rice

In a 2-quart shallow baking dish mix soup, water, rice, paprika and pepper. Place chicken on rice mixture. Sprinkle with additional paprika and pepper. Cover. Bake at 375° for 45 minutes or until done. Serves 4.

Joan Johnson

CHICKEN & STUFFING BAKE

4 c. Pepperidge Farm herb stuffing, seasoned
4-6 skinless, boneless chicken breast halves
1 (10¾-oz.) can cream of mushroom soup
⅓ c. milk
1 T. chopped fresh parsley

Mix stuffing, 1¼ cups boiling water and 4 tablespoons margarine. Spoon stuffing across center of 3-quart shallow dish. Place chicken on each side of stuffing. Sprinkle paprika over chicken. Mix soup, milk and parsley. Pour over chicken. Bake covered at 400° for 30 minutes or until chicken is no longer pink.

Joan Johnson

CHICKEN AND DUMPLINGS

1 whole chicken or 4 lg. chicken breasts
2 c. sifted all-purpose flour
1 tsp. salt
4 tsp. baking powder
4 T. cooking oil
¾ c. milk
1 whole chicken or 4 lg. chicken breasts, cooked and cut off bone

Sift dry ingredients. Combine milk and oil; add to dry ingredients and stir until all is mixed well. Roll out on floured surface very thin. Cut in strips and drop in boiling broth (stock). After all strips of dumplings have been added to broth and stirred frequently add chicken

(continued)

and continue to stir. If more salt is needed add to taste. Recipe can be doubled.

Joan Johnson

Comforting Chicken Casserole

1½ c. diced, cooked chicken
1½ c. cooked rice
1 c. chopped celery
½ c. chopped walnuts or pecans
1 can cream of chicken soup, undiluted
2 tsp. finely chopped onion
2 c. coarsely crumbled potato chips

½ tsp. black pepper
½ tsp. salt
1 T. lemon juice
¾ c. mayonnaise
¼ c. water
3 hard-boiled eggs, sliced

Combine first 10 ingredients in a large bowl. Combine mayonnaise and water; stir with a wire whisk until smooth. Add mayonnaise mixture to chicken mixture. Gently fold in egg slices. Spoon mixture into a greased 11 x 7-inch baking dish. Top with potato chips. Bake uncovered at 400° for 15 minutes or until bubbly. Yield 6 servings.

Patsy Pomeroy

Crazy Chicken or Turkey Pie

Inside Contents:

2 c. cut-up chicken or turkey
½ tsp. salt
1 c. shredded Swiss or sharp cheddar cheese

½ c. chopped onions
1 sm. can mushroom stems & pieces
3 eggs

Pie Shell:

1½ c. milk
¾ c. Bisquick

¼ tsp. poultry seasoning

Beat pie shell ingredients in blender until smooth. Pour over contents in pie plate and bake for 30-35 minutes in 400° oven. Pie is done when knife inserted in pie comes out clean.

Connie Cullers

CHICKEN TETRAZINNI

2 cans cream of chicken soup
1 can cream of celery soup
1 c. shredded cheddar cheese
1 c. shredded mozzarella cheese
1 chicken
8 oz. spaghetti

Boil chicken and remove skin, debone. Cook spaghetti in broth from chicken. Mix together chicken, spaghetti and soups in a large casserole dish. Sprinkle cheeses on top and bake at 350° for about 30 minutes.

Patsy Pomeroy

POPPY SEED CHICKEN

Boil 4 boneless chicken breasts for 1½ hours until very tender. Mix with:

1 can cream of chicken soup
1 (8-oz.) ctn. sour cream
1 sm. pkg. slivered almonds

Put in buttered casserole dish. Spread poppy seed and crumble Ritz crackers on top. Drizzle with butter and bake at 350° for 25 minutes.

Connie Cullers

SOUTHERN FRIED CHICKEN

1 whole chicken
1 c. all-purpose flour
Salt and pepper
2½ c. vegetable oil
1 brown paper bag

Wash and cut up whole chicken (separating leg from thigh and cutting breast into 2 pieces). I think the whole fresh chicken tastes best. In a cast-iron skillet heat vegetable oil until a pinch of flour dropped in sizzles. Place flour in brown paper bag. Salt and pepper chicken and place in bag. Shake until well coated. Add to hot grease and brown lightly each piece all over turning regularly. Reduce heat to medium-high and continue turning each piece until golden brown all over. Remove from grease with tongs and place on plate with paper towels to drain off excess oil.

Patsy Pomeroy

Family Chili

1 lb. ground beef
1 med. onion, chopped
Salt and pepper to taste
Grated cheddar cheese

1 can whole tomatoes
1 can Bush's best chili beans
1½ T. Mexene chili powder
1 c. water

Brown ground beef in large pot with chopped onion. Season with salt, pepper and chili powder stirring constantly until nice and brown. Add can of Bush's chili beans. Add 1 cup of water. Chop up canned tomatoes and add along with juice to other ingredients. Simmer for about 30 minutes until flavors are well blended. Sprinkle grated cheese on top of each bowl. Serve with saltine crackers.

Patsy Pomeroy

Ham and Egg Quiche

4 eggs
½ tsp. pepper
½ tsp. salt
¼ tsp. baking powder

½ c. milk
2 c. diced ham
1 c. grated cheese
1 unbaked pie shell

Bake eggs slightly, add salt, milk, baking powder and pepper. Mix in ham and cheese. Pour into pie shell and bake in 425° oven until center is firm. Over each slice melt mozzarella.

Joan Johnson

Hamburger Casserole

Brown 2 pounds ground beef with small chopped onion and garlic salt, 2 teaspoons chili powder. Add to that 1 large can tomato sauce, cooked noodles (your choice), 1 small can English peas and 1 can drained kidney beans. Pour this mixture into casserole dish and top with a full layer of cheddar cheese. Bake at 375° until it bubbles.

Joan Johnson

Hamburger Stroganoff

½ c. minced onion
1 clove garlic, minced
¼ c. butter
2 T. flour
1 tsp. salt
¼ tsp. pepper

1 lb. fresh mushrooms or 1 (6-oz.)
can sliced mushrooms, drained
1 lb. ground beef
1 can cream of chicken soup,
undiluted
1 c. sour cream

Sauté onion and garlic in butter over medium heat. Add meat and brown. Add flour, salt, pepper and mushrooms. Cook for 5 minutes. Add soup; simmer uncovered for 10 minutes. Stir in sour cream. Heat through. Serve with noodles or rice. Makes 4 to 6 servings.

Patsy Pomeroy

Pomeroy's Favorite Lasagna

Meat Sauce:

1 lb. ground beef
¼ tsp. oregano
¼ tsp. basil
⅛ tsp. garlic salt
Salt and pepper to taste

1 (16-oz.) can tomato sauce
1 (16-oz.) can tomato wedges
1 (8-oz.) can tomato paste
2 T. minced onion

Cheeses:

Cottage cheese
Mozzarella cheese

Cheddar cheese

Lasagna noodles, cooked

Brown ground beef and drain fat. Add spices. Add tomato sauce, paste and wedges. Bring to boil then simmer while noodles are cooking. Layer as follows; noodles, meat sauce, cottage cheese, noodles, meat sauce, cheddar cheese, noodles, meat sauce, mozzarella cheese. Bake at 350° for 45 minutes or until cheese is nice and bubbly. Let sit for several minutes before slicing.

Patsy Pomeroy

Lasagna

Home-style Ragu spaghetti sauce
2 lbs. hamburger meat
Cottage cheese

Parmesan cheese
Mozzarella cheese
Noodles

(continued)

Brown 2 pounds hamburger meat in skillet. Add home-style Ragu spaghetti sauce and mix well. Cook noodles and drain off water. Layer bottom of lasagna pan with some of sauce mixture. Add Parmesan cheese, then spread cottage cheese over top, then mozzarella cheese, then layer noodles. Start over again with sauce and other layerings. Top with mozzarella cheese and bake until bubbly.

Joan Johnson

MEAT LOAF

1½ lbs. ground beef
½ onion, chopped
½ c. unseasoned bread crumbs
1 egg, slightly beaten
1 can whole tomatoes
2 stalks celery, chopped
2 slices bread, toasted
Salt and pepper to taste

Take whole package of ground beef and mix in salt and pepper. Make a bowl shape out of it. In center place chopped onion and celery. Add chopped whole tomatoes and reserve juice in can. Crumble toasted bread and add to mixture with bread crumbs. Add beaten egg and mix all together with hands and form nice oval loaf. Place in meat loaf pan, pour remaining juice from canned tomatoes on top. Bake at 325° for approximately 1 hour.

Patsy Pomeroy

MEXICAN DINNER

1 lb. ground beef, browned & drained
1 tsp. salt
2 tsp. chili powder
¼ tsp. Tabasco pepper sauce
1½ c. chopped onion
2 c. kidney beans, undrained
1 (6-oz.) can tomato paste
Chopped lettuce
1 med. tomato, finely chopped
½-1 c. Monterey Jack, cheddar or American cheese

Combine all above ingredients except lettuce, tomato and cheese. Mix thoroughly. Spoon into Krazy Crust. Bake for 20 to 30 minutes until crust is deep golden brown. Sprinkle with lettuce, tomato and cheese. Serve with taco sauce if desired.

Joan Johnson

Pepper Steak with Rice

1½ lbs. sirloin steak, cut in ⅛-inch thick strips
1 T. paprika
2 cloves garlic, crushed
2 T. butter or margarine
1 c. sliced green onions with tops
2 green peppers, cut into strips
2 lg. fresh tomatoes, diced
1 c. beef broth
¼ c. water
2 T. cornstarch
2 T. soy sauce
3 c. cooked rice

Sprinkle steak with paprika and set aside while preparing other ingredients. Brown garlic in butter and add steak, onions and green peppers. Continue cooking until vegetables are wilted. Add tomatoes and broth; cover and simmer on low heat for about 15 minutes. Blend water with cornstarch and soy sauce; stir into steak. Cook until thickened. Serve over rice.

Joan Johnson

Favorite Pot Roast

1 Angus beef pot roast
6 sm. red potatoes

Salt and pepper roast. Use a little meat tenderizer all over. Place in roasting pot and brown on all sides over high heat turning until complexly brown using long handled fork. Add water to pot to cover roast and reduce heat to simmer. Add peeled and cut-up potatoes and cover to simmer for about 3 to 4 hours. Make a gravy for roast using 1½ tablespoons all-purpose flour in skillet. Let flour brown over medium heat stirring constantly. Add a little salt and pepper. Add juice from roast when flour is nice and brown. Stir until thickened and serve over roast.

Patsy Pomeroy

Salmon Croquette

1 can salmon
1 egg, slightly beaten
1 c. cornmeal
Vegetable oil

In a bowl break up salmon with fork. Add cornmeal and mix well. Add egg and mix together with hands. Form patties and fry in hot oil until nice and brown. Serve with catsup or seafood cocktail.

Patsy Pomeroy

Sausage Rice Casserole

2 lbs. hot or sweet Italian
  sausage, cut into ½-inch pieces
1 lg. green pepper slices in ¼-inch
  strips
1 med. onion, chopped
1 jar Ragu spaghetti sauce with
  mushrooms
3 c. cooked rice
½ tsp. fennel seed
1 can red kidney beans, drained
2 T. Parmesan cheese
¼ tsp. garlic powder
1½ c. shredded mozzarella cheese
Salt and pepper to taste

In a large skillet brown sausage on all sides. Add pepper and onion; sauté until almost tender. Drain. Add remaining ingredients except mozzarella cheese; mix well. Spoon into 9 x 13-inch baking dish. Top with cheese. Bake for 30 minutes or until bubbly at 350°.

Joan Johnson

Florida Seafood Casserole

3 c. cooked rice
½ lb. crab
½ lb. shrimp
⅓ c. green onions
1 tsp. salt
1 dash pepper
¼ c. butter
¼ c. flour
1 c. sharp cheddar cheese
6 oz. water chestnuts
2 T. lemon juice
1 c. milk
1 c. half & half
2 tsp. pimentos

Cook rice, heat oven to 350°. Chop shrimp and crab meat in bite-size pieces. Melt butter in skillet and sauté onions in butter until tender. Stir in salt and pepper, flour, half & half and milk; stir until thickened. Add lemon juice, drained canned water chestnuts, rice, chopped pimentos, crab and shrimp. Pour into oiled 1½-quart casserole. Sprinkle with grated cheese and bake for 25 minutes.

Connie Cullers

Shepherd's Pie

1 lb. ground beef
¼ med. onion, chopped
6 med. potatoes, boiled & mashed
  using salt, butter & little milk
2 carrots, peeled & cut up
1 c. sliced mushrooms
1 pkg. brown gravy mix
1 c. sharp cheddar cheese,
  shredded

Brown ground beef with chopped onions and drain off fat. Set aside. Cook carrots in pot on top of stove. Sauté mushrooms in a skillet

(continued)

with butter. Prepare mashed potatoes. Prepare gravy using package directions. Add to ground beef along with carrots and mushrooms. Cover and simmer over medium heat for a few minutes until thickened. Place beef mixture into a casserole dish and cover with mashed potatoes. Smooth out top of potatoes and cover with shredded cheese. Bake in oven at 350° until cheese is melted.

Tip: You may add English peas, green beans or corn if desired.

Patsy Pomeroy

SPAGHETTI MEAT SAUCE

1 lb. ground beef
½ c. onion
1 bay leaf
1 (1-lb.) can tomatoes
1½ tsp. oregano
2 tsp. garlic
1½ tsp. salt
1 (1-lb.) can tomato sauce

In a skillet brown 1 pound of ground beef with ½ cup of onion. Drain and add 2 teaspoons garlic, 1 (1-pound) can of tomatoes, 1 (1-pound) can of tomato sauce, 1 bay leaf and 1½ teaspoons of oregano. Simmer for 2½ hours or until sauce is thick. Remove bay leaf and serve over hot spaghetti.

Joan Johnson

SPAGHETTI PIE

6 oz. dry spaghetti
2 T. butter
⅓ c. grated Parmesan cheese
3 eggs, lightly beaten
1 lb. ground beef
1 c. ricotta cheese
1 (28-oz.) jar spaghetti sauce
½ c. shredded mozzarella cheese

Cook and drain pasta. Stir in butter. In a bowl beat together Parmesan and eggs; then fold into pasta. Press the pasta lightly into the bottom and sides of buttered 10-inch pie pan to form a crust. Brown the ground beef and drain fat. Spread the ricotta cheese over the spaghetti. Stir the ground beef into the spaghetti sauce and spoon mixture over the pie. Sprinkle mozzarella on top. Bake uncovered for 20 minutes at 350° or until nice and bubbly. Cut into wedges to serve.

Patsy Pomeroy

SPARERIBS AND SAUERKRAUT

2 lbs. spareribs
1 qt. sauerkraut
1/8 tsp. pepper
1/2 tsp. salt

Cut spareribs into pieces lying flat in the Dutch oven. Brown well on both sides. Add seasoning. Lift meat and place on top of kraut. Cover and cook for 30 minutes.

Joan Johnson

GREEK SPINACH AND CHEESE PIE

1/2 (1-lb.) pkg. prepared phyllo or strudel pastry leaves (16 sheets 12 x 15 inch)
1/4 c. butter or margarine
1/2 c. finely chopped onion
3 (10-oz.) pkgs. frozen, chopped spinach, thawed & well drained
3 eggs
1/2 lb. feta cheese, crumbled
1/4 c. chopped parsley
2 T. chopped fresh dill
1 tsp. salt
1/8 tsp. pepper
3/4 c. butter or margarine, melted

Preheat oven to 350°. Let pastry leaves warm to room temperature according to directions on package. In 1/4 cup hot butter in medium skillet, sauté onions until golden, about 5 minutes. Add spinach, stir to combine with onion. Remove from heat. In a large bowl beat eggs with rotary beater. With wooden spoon stir in cheese, parsley, dill, salt, pepper and spinach/onion mixture; mix well. Brush a 9 x 13 x 2-inch baking pan lightly with some of the melted butter. In bottom of baking pan, layer 8 phyllo pastry leaves, one by one brushing top of each with melted butter. Spread evenly with spinach mixture. Cover with 8 more leaves brushing each with butter, pour any remaining melted butter over top. Using scissors trim of any uneven edges of pastry. Cut through top pastry layer on diagonal then cut in opposite direction to form about 9 (3-inch) diamonds. Bake for 30-35 minutes or until top crust is puffy and golden. Serve warm.

Patsy Pomeroy

PORK CHOPS AND PEAS

8 pork chops
1 T. cooking oil
1 onion, sliced
4 lg. potatoes, peeled & sliced
Salt and pepper
1 can Le Sueur peas, undrained

(continued)

Brown pork chops in oil in electric fry pan. Add onion and sauté a bit. Add potatoes and sauté, add more oil. Pour peas over all. Cover and simmer for about an hour at 325°. Serves 4.

Patsy Pomeroy

SHRIMP CASSEROLE

1 lb. shrimp
1 c. celery
1 c. cottage cheese
1 dash Tabasco sauce
1 sm. jar diced pimento

½ tsp. salt and pepper
1 tsp. Worcestershire sauce
1 c. Hellmann's mayonnaise
1 sm. onion, chopped
Ritz crackers

Mix all ingredients and put them in a buttered casserole and sprinkle Ritz crackers on top. Bake at 350° for 30 minutes or until bubbly.

Connie Cullers

CHEESE GRITS AND SHRIMP CASSEROLE

Favorite brand grits
¼ c. cream
Italian sausage
White wine
1 c. shrimp, peeled & deveined

Shredded provolone cheese
Shredded mozzarella cheese
Fresh mushrooms
Chopped scallions
Little bacon, fried & crumbled

Cook grits according to directions. (Some people like to cook their grits with a little cream and chicken broth instead of the water called for in directions.) Add grated mozzarella and provolone cheese to grits before they are done and let melt. In a separate saucepan cook sausage and drain. Add mushrooms, scallions, bacon, white wine and cream. Simmer. Add shrimp and let cook through for a few minutes. Add ingredients to grits and cheese mixture and serve in a casserole dish.

Patsy Pomeroy

EASY SHRIMP CREOLE

½ c. diced celery
¼ c. minced onion
¼ c. diced green pepper
3 T. butter
1 T. all-purpose flour
1 tsp. salt
1 tsp. sugar
Hot cooked rice

1 (16-oz.) can tomatoes
1 bay leaf
1 sprig parsley
¾ lb. (1½ c.) shrimp, cleaned & cooked
¼ tsp. Worcestershire sauce
1 dash pepper

Sauté celery, onion and green pepper in butter in saucepan until tender but not browned. Blend in flour, salt, sugar and pepper. Stir in tomatoes; add bay leaf and parsley. Simmer for 30 minutes. Remove bay leaf and parsley. Add shrimp and Worcestershire sauce and heat thoroughly. Serve over hot cooked rice.

Patsy Pomeroy

STUFFED SHELLS

1 box lg. shell pasta
1 lg. ctn. ricotta cheese
2 eggs
1 lg. bag mozzarella cheese

2 jars spaghetti sauce
1 sm. bag shredded Swiss cheese
1 bag sliced provolone cheese

Cook shells according to package directions. Let cool for about 10 minutes or until touchable. Meanwhile combine the eggs, ricotta and Swiss cheese together until well blended. In a 9 x 13-inch pan pour enough sauce to coat the bottom. Stuff shells with cheese mixture and place in pan forming rows. When the pan is full cover shells completely with sauce. Top with provolone and mozzarella cheeses. Bake at 375° for 30 minutes or until cheeses are bubbly.

Patsy Pomeroy

TAMALE PIE

1 lb. ground meat
1 onion, chopped
1 can tomato sauce

1 can Bush's chili hot beans
½ c. water
Cornbread mix

This recipe is best used in a cast-iron skillet. Brown ground meat, add onions and sauté with meat. Add chili beans and water. Add tomato sauce and simmer for about 10 minutes. Mix cornbread mix

(continued)

according to directions. Pour in middle of sauce mixture. Bake at 350° until cornbread is nice and brown. Serves 4.

Patsy Pomeroy

VEAL SCALOPPINI

8 thinly sliced veal scaloppini (about 1½ lbs.)
½ c. all-purpose flour

6 T. butter
Parsley
Lemon slices

Pound veal until thin and tender. Coat with flour and sauté in butter in large skillet for about 10 minutes, turning to brown both sides. Garnish with lemon slices and parsley.

Tip: I add a little water and flour mixture to drippings in skillet. Season with salt and pepper and serve over scaloppini.

Patsy Pomeroy

Recipe Favorites

Recipe Favorites

Breads & Rolls

Helpful Hints

- When baking bread, a small dish of water in the oven will keep the crust from getting too hard or brown.

- Use shortening, not margarine or oil, to grease pans when baking bread. Margarine and oil absorb more readily into the dough.

- To make self-rising flour, mix 4 cups flour, 2 teaspoons salt, and 2 tablespoons baking powder. Store in a tightly covered container.

- One scant tablespoon of bulk yeast is equal to one packet of yeast.

- Hot water kills yeast. One way to test for the correct temperature is to pour the water over your wrist. If you cannot feel hot or cold, the temperature is just right.

- When in doubt, always sift flour before measuring.

- Use bread flour for baking heavier breads, such as mixed grain, pizza doughs, bagels, etc.

- When baking in a glass pan, reduce the oven temperature by 25°.

- When baking bread, you can achieve a finer texture if you use milk. Water makes a coarser bread.

- Fill an empty salt shaker with flour to quickly and easily dust a bread pan or work surface.

- For successful quick breads, do not overmix the dough. Mix only until combined. An overmixed batter creates tough and rubbery muffins, biscuits, and quick breads.

- Muffins can be eaten warm. Most other quick breads taste better the next day. Nut breads are better if stored 24 hours before serving.

- Nuts, shelled or unshelled, keep best and longest when stored in the freezer. Unshelled nuts crack more easily when frozen. Nuts can be used directly from the freezer.

- Enhance the flavor of nuts, such as almonds, walnuts, and pecans, by toasting them before using in recipes. Place nuts on a baking sheet and bake at 300° for 5–8 minutes or until slightly browned.

- Overripe bananas can be frozen until it's time to bake. Store them unpeeled in a plastic bag.

- The freshness of eggs can be tested by placing them in a large bowl of cold water; if they float, do not use them.

Breads & Rolls

Apple Muffins

Combine the following in a bowl:

1½ c. firmly packed light brown sugar
⅔ c. vegetable oil
1 egg

In another bowl combine:

1 c. buttermilk
1 tsp. baking soda
1 tsp. salt
1 tsp. vanilla

Add milk mixture to sugar mixture alternately with 2½ cups flour; mix well after each addition. Fold in:

1½ c. diced Granny Smith apples
½ c. chopped pecans

Pour into greased and floured muffin tins. Sprinkle with ⅓ cup sugar combined with 1 tablespoon melted butter. Bake at 325° for 30 minutes or until cake tester comes out clean. Makes 24.

Patsy Pomeroy

Apricot Banana Bread

⅓ c. butter, softened
1 c. mashed ripe bananas
1¼ c. all-purpose flour
1 tsp. baking powder
¾ c. (6 oz.) chopped dried apricots
⅔ c. sugar
¼ c. buttermilk
½ tsp. soda
1 c. 100% bran cereal, not flakes
2 eggs
½ tsp. salt
½ c. chopped walnuts

Cream butter and sugar in mixing bowl. Combine bananas and buttermilk. Combine the flour and other dry ingredients; add to creamed mixture alternating with banana mixture. Stir in bran, apricots and nuts. Pour into greased 9 x 5 x 3-inch loaf pan. Bake for 55 to 60 minutes or until done at 350°. Cool, then remove from pan.

Joan Johnson

Banana Nut Bread

1/3 c. shortening or oil
1/2 c. sugar
2 eggs
1 3/4 c. sifted all-purpose flour
1 tsp. baking powder
1/2 tsp. soda
1/2 tsp. salt
1 c. mashed bananas
1/2 c. chopped nuts

Grease and flour 9 1/2 x 5 x 3-inch loaf pan. Cream shortening and sugar; add eggs one at a time. Beat well. Sift dry ingredients together; add to cream mixture, alternating with banana, blending well after each addition. Stir in nuts. Pour into loaf pan, bake for 40 to 45 minutes until done at 350°. Cool.

Joan Johnson

Banana Walnut Muffins

3 c. Oat Bran Options cereal
3 med. ripe bananas, mashed
3 egg whites
2 T. milk
1/4 c. chopped walnuts
2 T. oil
1 c. flour
2 T. packed brown sugar
1 T. baking powder

In a medium bowl combine cereal, bananas, egg whites, milk and oil. Let stand for 5 minutes. In a large bowl combine flour, sugar and baking powder. Add cereal mixture to flour mixture stirring just until moistened. Spoon into prepared muffin cups. Sprinkle with nuts. Bake at 400° for about 20 minutes. Makes 12.

Joan Johnson

Blueberry Muffins

2 c. all-purpose flour
1/2 tsp. salt
1 c. sugar
1 tsp. vanilla
2-2 1/2 c. fresh or frozen blueberries
1 T. sugar with 1/4 tsp. ground nutmeg
2 tsp. baking powder
1/2 c. butter, softened
2 lg. eggs
1/2 c. milk

Sift first 3 ingredients together. Cream remaining ingredients except for milk. Add flour mixture to creamed mixture alternating with the milk. Fold in the blueberries. Spoon dough into greased muffin cups

(continued)

then sprinkle top with nutmeg sugar. Bake at 375° for 25 to 30 minutes. The nutmeg can be added into the dough if desired.

Joan Johnson

BRAN MUFFINS

1½ c. all-purpose flour
3 tsp. baking soda
½ tsp. salt
½ c. sugar

1½ c. Kellogg's All Bran cereal
1 egg
1¼ c. milk
⅓ c. shortening or oil

Stir together flour, baking soda, salt and sugar. Set aside and add to shortening. Beat well and then add to flour mixture stirring only until combined. Fill greased muffin pan cups. Bake at 400° for 25 minutes.

Joan Johnson

CRANBERRY NUT BREAD

2 c. sifted all-purpose flour
1 c. sugar
1½ tsp. baking powder
1 tsp. salt
¼ c. shortening
¾ c. orange juice
1 c. fresh cranberries, coarsely chopped or 1 c. well drained whole cranberries

½ c. chopped walnuts or pecans
½ tsp. soda
1 egg, well beaten
1 tsp. grated orange peel

Grease and flour 9 x 5-inch loaf pan. Sift dry ingredients into a large bowl. Cut in shortening. Combine egg, orange juice and peel and add to dry ingredients mixing just to moisten. Fold in berries and nuts. Pour into pan and bake for about 1 hour at 350° until done. Cool in pan, then remove from pan.

Joan Johnson

CRUNCHY CHEESE BISCUITS

½ c. butter, softened
1 c. flour
1 c. shredded sharp cheddar cheese, softened

½ tsp. salt
Tabasco to taste
1 c. rice cereal

(continued)

Blend all ingredients together except cereal by hand in a bowl until thoroughly mixed. Work in cereal. pinch off into tiny balls. Place on ungreased cookie sheet, press down with fork. Bake at 325° for about 10 minutes or until faintly colored. Yields about 48 balls.

Joan Johnson

DATE NUT BREAD

1 (1-lb.) pkg. dates	1 lb. pecans
1 c. plain flour	3 eggs
1 tsp. baking powder	1 c. sugar
1 T. vanilla	1 tsp. salt

Break pecans, chop dates and mix together. Sift flour and baking powder and sprinkle over date-nut mixture. Separate eggs and beat yolk. Gradually add sugar, beating well. Add vanilla, fold in dates and nuts; then fold in stiffly beaten egg whites into which salt has been added. Pour in greased wax paper-lined loaf pan. Bake for 40-50 minutes at 325°.

Patsy Pomeroy

QUICK LEMONADE BREAD

1 T. frozen lemonade concentrate, thawed	2 eggs
1/2 c. shortening	2 T. baking powder
1 c. sugar	1/2 c. milk
1 1/2 c. all-purpose flour	1/3 c. frozen lemonade concentrate, thawed

Combine all ingredients except 1/3 cup frozen lemonade, thawed, in a large bowl. Blend well. Beat for 3 minutes at medium speed with hand mixer. Pour into greased loaf pan and bake for 50 to 60 minutes at 350°. Loosen bread from edges of pan. Pour 1/3 cup concentrate over bread. Cool, remove from pan.

Patsy Pomeroy

QUICK MAYONNAISE ROLLS

2 c. self-rising flour	1 c. sweet milk
4 T. mayonnaise	

(continued)

Pour cup of milk in mixing bowl, add mayonnaise. Beat for 2 minutes. Add flour gradually. Prepare greased muffin pan and spoon in batter. Place in preheated 350° oven and bake for 15-20 minutes. Will make 12 rolls.

Patsy Pomeroy

Hot Mexican Bread

1½ c. yellow cornmeal
1 T. baking powder
2 T. chopped green pepper
1 c. cream-style corn
1-2 jalapeño peppers, chopped

1 tsp. salt
2 eggs, beaten
1 c. sour cream
¼ c. vegetable oil
1 c. shredded cheddar cheese

Combine cornmeal, salt and baking powder; mix well. Stir in remaining ingredients except cheese. Pour half the batter into a hot, greased 10½-inch iron skillet; sprinkle evenly with half the cheese. Pour the remaining batter over cheese; top with remaining cheese. Bake at 350° for 35 to 40 minutes.

Joan Johnson

Oatmeal Muffins

1½ c. any pancake mix
½ c. packed brown sugar
1 c. milk
¼ c. oil
⅓ c. raisins

1 c. uncooked Quaker oats
1½ tsp. cinnamon
1 egg
½ c. peeled, chopped apple

Combine pancake mix, oats, brown sugar and cinnamon. Add remaining ingredients; mix just until dry ingredients are moistened. Fill greased muffin cups ¾ full. Bake at 425° for 15 to 20 minutes. Makes 1 dozen.

Joan Johnson

PINEAPPLE NUT BREAD

1½ c. firmly packed brown sugar
½ c. shortening
2 eggs
4 c. sifted flour
2 tsp. baking soda
¾ tsp. salt
1 (6-oz.) can frozen orange juice concentrate, thawed
1 (15¼-oz.) can Del Monte crushed pineapple with juice
1 c. chopped walnuts

Cream sugar and shortening until light and fluffy. Add eggs; beat well. Sift together flour, baking soda and salt. Alternately add dry ingredients and orange concentrate to creamed mixture; mix well after each addition. Stir in pineapple and nuts. Turn into 2 greased and floured 8½ x 4½-inch loaf pans. Bake at 350° for 50 to 60 minutes. Remove from pans. Cool on rack. Makes 2 loaves.

Patsy Pomeroy

PUMPKIN BREAD

2¾ c. sugar
2 sticks margarine
3 eggs
2 c. pumpkin
2¾ c. sifted all-purpose flour
1 tsp. baking soda
2 tsp. baking powder
1 tsp. cinnamon
1 T. vanilla
1 tsp. nutmeg
1 tsp. cloves
¼ tsp. salt
1 c. chopped nuts

Cream sugar and margarine. Add eggs one at a time. Add dry ingredients after sifting all together. Mix well. Add pumpkin and vanilla and nuts; mix together well. Pour into loaf pan or pans and bake for 1 hour at 325°.

Joan Johnson

STICKY BUNS

1 loaf frozen bread dough, thawed in refrigerator overnight
1 stick plus 1 T. butter, melted
½ c. chopped pecans
½ c. firmly packed brown sugar
½ c. sugar
1 T. cinnamon

Mix well together brown sugar, sugar and cinnamon and set aside. Cut dough crosswise in ½-inch pieces. Then slice down center lengthwise. Dip pieces of bread dough first in butter then in chopped pecans and then in sugar mixture. Arrange in an angle food cake pan. Let rise

(continued)

in oven that has been turned on to low warm for 30-45 minutes. Cover with dry towel. Then bake at 350° for 30-45 minutes.

Patsy Pomeroy

STRAWBERRY NUT BREAD

3 c. flour
1 tsp. baking soda
1 tsp. salt
3 tsp. cinnamon
2 c. sugar
4 eggs, well beaten
1¼ c. vegetable oil
1¼ c. chopped walnuts or pecans
1 (10-oz.) pkg. frozen strawberries, thawed
Powdered sugar (opt.)

Stir dry ingredients together. Combine the rest in a separate bowl. Add the liquid mixture to the dry mixture. Stir it together carefully just enough to blend the ingredients. Fill 5 small greased loaf pans no more than ¾ full. Bake at 350° for 45 to 50 minutes. They are done when a toothpick inserted in the middle comes out clean. Cool in the pans. Sprinkle with powdered sugar if desired.

Tip: You can use 2 large loaf pans or 3 medium loaf pans and bake at 350° for 55-60 minutes, again test timing with a toothpick. It will generally take a bit longer than the recipe states.

Patsy Pomeroy

PULL-APART VEGETABLE BREAD

3 cans biscuits
½ lb. fried bacon
¾ c. bell pepper
¾ c. onion
½ c. Parmesan cheese
2 sticks butter

Cut the biscuits in quarters. Crumble bacon. Cook onion and pepper in 2 sticks butter. Mix all ingredients together. Put in unbuttered bundt pan. Bake for 20 minutes at 400° or 30 minutes at 350°.

Patsy Pomeroy

ZUCCHINI NUT BREAD

3½ c. flour
2 c. sugar
1 tsp. cinnamon
2 c. grated, unpeeled zucchini
1 c. walnuts (opt.)
1½ tsp. baking soda
¾ tsp. baking powder
1 tsp. salt
4 eggs
1 c. vegetable oil

(continued)

In a large bowl mix all dry ingredients. In a medium bowl beat eggs and oil until smooth. Pour liquid mixture over the dry mixture and stir until moistened. Turn into 2 greased bread pans (9 x 5-inch). Bake at 350° for 1 to 1½ hours. Insert toothpick in center to determine if the bread is done. Cool pans for about 10 minutes then remove bread from pans and cool right side up on wire racks. Makes 2 loaves.

Patsy Pomeroy

Recipe Favorites

Desserts

Helpful Hints

- Keep eggs at room temperature to create greater volume when whipping egg whites for meringue.

- Pie dough can be frozen. Roll dough out between sheets of plastic wrap, stack in a pizza box, and keep the box in the freezer. Defrost in the fridge and use as needed. Use within 2 months.

- Place your pie plate on a cake stand when ready to flute the edges of the pie. The cake stand will make it easier to turn the pie plate, and you won't have to stoop over.

- When making decorative pie edges, use a spoon for a scalloped edge. Use a fork to make crosshatched and herringbone patterns.

- When cutting butter into flour for pastry dough, the process is easier if you cut the butter into small pieces before adding it to the flour.

- Pumpkin and other custard-style pies are done when they jiggle slightly in the middle. Fruit pies are done when the pastry is golden, juices bubble, and fruit is tender.

- Keep the cake plate clean while frosting by sliding 6-inch strips of waxed paper under each side of the cake. Once the cake is frosted and the frosting is set, pull the strips away, leaving a clean plate.

- Create a quick decorating tube to ice your cake with chocolate. Put chocolate in a heat-safe, zipper-lock plastic bag. Immerse it in simmering water until the chocolate is melted. Snip off the tip of one corner, and squeeze the chocolate out of the bag.

- Achieve professionally decorated cakes with a silky, molten look by blow-drying the frosting with a hair dryer until the frosting melts slightly.

- To ensure that you have equal amounts of batter in each pan when making a layered cake, use a kitchen scale to measure the weight.

- Prevent cracking in your cheesecake by placing a shallow pan of hot water on the bottom oven rack and keeping the oven door shut during baking.

- A cheesecake needs several hours to chill and set.

- For a perfectly cut cheesecake, dip the knife into hot water and clean it after each cut. You can also hold a length of dental floss taut and pull it down through the cheesecake to make a clean cut across the diameter of the cake.

Desserts

Apple Cake

3 1/3 c. apples, chopped
2 c. sugar
1 c. oil
2 eggs
1 c. nuts
3 c. flour

2 tsp. soda
1 tsp. salt
2 tsp. cinnamon
1 tsp. nutmeg
1 tsp. allspice

Mix all ingredients together and bake in floured bundt pan. Bake at 350° for 50 minutes. After cake has been taken out of oven poke holes in top and pour sauce over top.

Sauce For Cake:

1 stick butter
1 c. sugar
1/2 tsp. soda

1 T. Karo white syrup
1/2 tsp. vanilla

Bring all ingredients to a boil and boil hard for 2 minutes. Pour hot sauce over cake and into poked holes.

Patsy Pomeroy

Fresh Apple Cake

2 c. sugar
1 tsp. vanilla
1 1/2 c. oil
4 eggs
2-3 c. finely chopped apples

1 c. chopped pecans
1 tsp. soda
2 tsp. nutmeg
1 tsp. cinnamon
3 c. plain sifted flour

Mix first 4 ingredients and cream well. Add flour and spices to the cream mixture. Add apples and mix into mixture. Stir in pecans. Bake for 1 hour at 350° in a tube pan (greased and floured).

Topping:

1 1/2 c. brown sugar
1 stick butter or margarine

1/2 c. pecans, chopped
3 tsp. milk

(continued)

Place all ingredients in saucepan and bring to a boil. Cook until soft ball stage. Spoon topping over warm cake.

Joan Johnson

Applesauce Cake

½ c. shortening
½ c. packed brown sugar
½ c. granulated sugar
2 eggs
1 tsp. soda
1 tsp. salt
1 tsp. baking powder

1 tsp. cinnamon
½ tsp. nutmeg
¼ tsp. cloves
1½ c. applesauce
2 c. sifted all-purpose flour
½ c. walnuts
½ c. raisins

Cream shortening and sugar until light and fluffy. Add eggs, beat well. Sift together all dry ingredients; add to cream mixture alternating with the applesauce. Beat well after each addition. Stir in nuts and raisins. Spread batter into greased 13 x 9½ x 2-inch pan. Bake at 350° for 35 to 40 minutes.

Connie Cullers

Banana Cake

1 c. shortening
2 c. sugar
2 eggs
2 c. mashed ripe bananas
1 tsp. vanilla

3 c. sifted cake flour
1 c. chopped pecans
¼ c. buttermilk
1 tsp. baking soda
1 tsp. salt

Grease and flour 2 (8-inch) square or 2 (9-inch) round cake pans. Cream shortening and sugar until light and fluffy. Add eggs one at a time beating well after each one. Add bananas and vanilla; mix well. Sift together dry ingredients slowly beat into creamed mixture with buttermilk, beginning and ending with dry ingredients. Stir in pecans. Pour into prepared pans. Bake for 40-45 minutes at 350° or until cake pulls away from sides of the pan. Cool and frost with Banana Frosting. Cake may also be baked in a 9 x 13 x 2-inch pan for 50-60 minutes.

Banana Frosting:

¼ c. butter or margarine
½ c. mashed bananas

1 tsp. lemon juice
1 lb. confectioners' sugar

(continued)

Combine butter, mashed bananas, lemon juice and sugar. Cream butter until fluffy. Stir in bananas and lemon juice; blend well. Gradually beat in sugar until frosting is of spreading consistency.

Joan Johnson

Banana Frosting
(2nd Option)

2 (8-oz.) pkgs. cream cheese, softened
1 tsp. vanilla
2-3 T. milk

1 c. mashed bananas
Dash of salt
1 tsp. lemon juice
2 c. confectioners' sugar

Beat softened cream cheese, vanilla and salt until smooth. Gradually beat in confectioners' sugar and milk until thick. Mix mashed bananas and lemon juice together then add to other ingredients. Spread onto top and sides of one layer and then continue until all 3 layers are frosted.

Joan Johnson

Great Carrot Cake

1½ c. chopped nuts
3 c. sifted all-purpose flour
3 tsp. baking powder
1 tsp. salt
2 c. packed brown sugar
4 lg. eggs

1 c. oil
1½ tsp. cinnamon
1 tsp. nutmeg
¼ tsp. cloves
3 T. milk
3 c. grated carrots

Grease 3 cake pans well. Combine sugar, egg, oil and spices. Beat at high speed until well mixed. Add half of flour, baking powder and salt, stir until well blended. Add milk then remaining flour. Stir in carrots and nuts. Divide batter evenly in 3 pans. Bake for 25 minutes until cakes test done at 350°.

Cream Cheese Frosting:

16 oz. cream cheese, softened
1 tsp. vanilla

2-3 T. milk
4 c. confectioners' sugar

Beat cream cheese and vanilla until smooth. Gradually add sugar and milk until thick and spreading consistency. Spread on tops of 3 cake layers.

Joan Johnson

BEST CARROT CAKE

1½ c. oil
2 eggs
2 tsp. baking soda
1 can crushed pineapple
2 c. peeled, grated carrots
½ tsp. salt

1¾ c. sugar
2 c. all-purpose flour
¾ c. shredded coconut
1 c. chopped walnuts
3 tsp. cinnamon
1 tsp. cloves

Beat together oil, sugar and eggs until combined. In a bowl sift flour, soda, salt, cinnamon and cloves. Add to egg mixture mixing well. Drain the pineapple well and add them and the walnuts into the mixture. Blend well. Pour batter into greased and floured 9- or 10-inch cake pan. Bake at 350° for about 1 hour or until a pick inserted in center comes out clean. Let cake cool on rack.

Cream Cheese Frosting:

2 pkgs. cream cheese
1 c. powdered sugar

1 tsp. vanilla

Blend well. Split cake into 2 layers and cover with frosting while assembling. Sprinkle with coconut.

Joan Johnson

CHOCOLATE COCOA COLA CAKE

2 sticks margarine
3 T. cocoa
1 c. cola
Baker's Joy
½ c. buttermilk
1 tsp. soda

1½ c. mini marshmallows
3 eggs
1 tsp. vanilla
2 c. all-purpose flour
2 c. sugar

Spray a 9 x 13-inch pan with Baker's Joy. Bring the margarine, cocoa and the cola to a boiling point. Mix 2 cups all-purpose flour with 2 cups sugar. Pour the boiled mixture over the flour mixture and mix altogether. Add 1 teaspoon vanilla, 1 teaspoon baking soda, ½ cup buttermilk and 3 eggs. Stir in 1½ cups mini marshmallows. Pour into pan and bake for 30-35 minutes at 350°. **Frosting:** Bring to boiling point ½ cup butter, 3 tablespoons cocoa, 6 tablespoons cola. Pour over 1 box confectioners' sugar and mix well. Add 1 cup chopped pecans and pour over warm cake.

Joan Johnson

Chocolate Disappearing Cake

¼ c. butter
¼ c. shortening
2 c. sugar
1 tsp. vanilla
2 eggs
¾ cocoa

1¾ c. unsifted all-purpose flour
¾ tsp. baking powder
¾ tsp. baking soda
⅛ tsp. salt
1¾ c. milk

Generously grease and flour 2 (9-inch) round cake pans. Cream butter, shortening, sugar and vanilla until fluffy; blend in eggs. Combine cocoa, flour, baking powder, baking soda and salt in a bowl; add alternately with milk to batter. Blend well. Pour into pans, bake for 30 to 35 minutes or until done at 350°. Cool. Use your favorite cocoa frosting recipe.

Joan Johnson

Chocolate Sheet Cake

1¼ c. butter
½ c. unsweetened cocoa
2 c. unsifted flour
1 c. water
1½ c. packed brown sugar
1 tsp. baking soda
1 tsp. cinnamon

½ tsp. salt
1 (14-oz.) can sweetened
  condensed milk
2 eggs
1 tsp. vanilla
1 c. confectioners' sugar
1 c. chopped pecans

In a small saucepan melt 1 cup butter, stir in ¼ cup cocoa then water. Bring to a boil; remove from heat. In a large bowl combine flour, brown sugar, soda, cinnamon and salt. Add cocoa mixture; beat well. Stir in ⅓ cup condensed milk, eggs and vanilla. Pour into greased and floured 15 x 10-inch pan. Bake for 15 minutes or until cake springs back when touched. In a small saucepan melt remaining ¼ cup butter, stir in remaining ¼ cup cocoa and condensed milk. Stir in confectioners' sugar and nuts. Spread on warm cake. Bake at 350°.

Joan Johnson

Coconut Cake

Spray 3 round cake pans with Baker's Joy.

(continued)

1 c. milk
2 c. sugar
3 c. self-rising flour
4 eggs
1 tsp. vanilla
Milk from 1 fresh coconut

Mix all ingredients together, flour last. Pour into 3 pans. Bake until done. Punch holes in top of cake and pour coconut milk from fresh coconut into the holes. Bake at 350°. Frost with Seven Minute Frosting recipe found on page 102.

Joan Johnson

CREAM CARAMEL CAKE

2 sticks butter
3 c. granulated sugar
6 eggs
1 tsp. salt
2²/₃ c. all-purpose flour
¼ tsp. baking soda
1 (8-oz.) ctn. sour cream
1 T. vanilla

Cream butter and sugar until fluffy. Add eggs one at a time. Sift flour, salt and soda together. Alternate flour mix and sour cream to butter mixture. Add vanilla. Pour into 3 (9-inch) prepared pans. Bake for 25-35 minutes or until dozen. Cool then frost. Bake at 350°.

Caramel Frosting:

½ lb. butter
2 c. light brown sugar
4 c. confectioners' sugar
½ c. evaporated milk
½ tsp. vanilla

Melt butter, add brown sugar and milk then cook for 2 minutes over medium heat stirring constantly. Remove from heat then add vanilla and pour over confectioners' sugar. Beat until smooth. Let cool slightly. Frost layers and sides.

Joan Johnson

GERMAN CHOCOLATE CAKE

1 (4-oz.) pkg. Baker's German
  sweet chocolate
½ c. boiling water
1 c. margarine or butter
2 c. sugar
1 tsp. soda
½ tsp. salt
2½ c. sifted all-purpose flour
4 egg whites, stiffly beaten
4 egg yolks
1 tsp. vanilla
1 c. buttermilk

Melt chocolate in boiling water. Cool. Cream butter and sugar until fluffy. Add yolks one at a time. Blend in vanilla and chocolate. Sift flour with soda and salt; add alternately with buttermilk to chocolate

(continued)

mixture beating well after each addition until smooth. Fold in beaten egg whites. Pour into 3 (9-inch) cake pans which were greased and floured previously. Bake at 350° for 30 to 35 minutes. Cool. Frost tops only.

German Chocolate Frosting/Filling:

1 c. sugar
1 stick margarine
1 c. flaked coconut
1 c. chopped pecans

1 c. evaporated milk
3 egg yolks, beaten
1 tsp. vanilla

Cook all ingredients except nuts and coconut over medium heat until thickened; about 12 minutes. Add coconut and pecans. Cool until thick enough to spread, beating occasionally. Spread over tops of cakes.

Joan Johnson

GINGERBREAD

½ c. shortening
1¼ c. packed brown sugar
2 eggs
2 c. all-purpose flour

1 tsp. soda
¾ cinnamon
1½ tsp. ginger
1 c. milk

Cream ½ cup of shortening and 1¼ cups of packed brown sugar thoroughly. Add 2 eggs, beating until light. Alternately add 2 cups of sifted all-purpose flour, 1 teaspoon soda, ¾ cinnamon, 1½ teaspoons ginger, ½ teaspoon nutmeg, ¾ teaspoon salt and 1 cup of milk. Beat well after each addition. Pour batter into greased 8-inch square pan. Bake for at hour or until done at 350°.

Joan Johnson

GOOD MORNING CAKE

2 T. sugar
1 tsp. cinnamon
¼ c. chopped pecans

¼ c. caramel topping
2 (8-oz.) pkgs. refrigerated biscuits
⅓ c. margarine

Mix cinnamon with sugar and sprinkle over bottom of a round, greased 9-inch cake pan. Cover sugar with nuts and pour caramel topping over nuts. Dip biscuits in margarine and arrange overlapping

(continued)

in pan. Put 5 in outer circle and 5 in middle. Bake for 25 minutes; cool for 5 minutes and turn right side up onto plate. Bake at 350°.

Joan Johnson

HOT FUDGE PUDDING CAKE

1¼ c. sugar, divided
7 T. cocoa, divided
¼ tsp. salt
⅓ c. butter
½ c. light brown sugar

1 c. all-purpose flour
2 tsp. baking powder
½ c. milk
1½ tsp. vanilla
1¼ c. hot water

Combine ¾ cup sugar, flour, 3 tablespoons cocoa, baking powder and salt in mixing bowl. Blend in milk, melted butter and vanilla; beat until smooth. Pour batter into square pan (8 x 8 x 2 inch or 9 x 9 x 2 inch). In a small bowl combine remaining ½ cup sugar, brown sugar and remaining 4 tablespoons cocoa; sprinkle mixture evenly over batter. Pour hot water over top; do not stir. Bake for 40 minutes or until center is almost set. Let stand for 15 minutes; spoon into dessert dishes, spooning sauce from bottom of pan over top. Bake at 350°.

Joan Johnson

JAPANESE FRUITCAKE

2 sticks butter
1 c. milk
6 eggs, separated
1 tsp. cinnamon
1 tsp. nutmeg
¼ tsp. salt
1 c. raisins

2 c. sugar
3 c. sifted flour
1 tsp. vanilla
1 tsp. cloves
4 tsp. baking powder
1 c. pecans
1 c. grated coconut

Cream butter and sugar. Beat egg yolks, add to cream mix. Add milk and flour which has been sifted with spices and salt. Add raisins, nuts and coconut. Beat egg whites, fold in. Bake in 4 layer pans which have been sprayed with Baker's Joy for 20 to 25 minutes at 350°.

Filling:

2 oranges
¾ c. crushed pineapple
1½ c. boiling water

2 c. sugar
4 T. flour
1 c. grated coconut

(continued)

Peel oranges, cut into small pieces. Mix flour and sugar together; add water. Add orange pieces and pineapple. Cook until thick like honey stirring constantly. Add coconut. Cool. Spread on layers of cake.

Joan Johnson

Southern Lane Cake

1 c. butter
3¼ c. flour
¾ tsp. salt
3½ tsp. baking soda
2 c. sugar

½ c. milk
½ evaporated milk
8 egg whites
1 tsp. vanilla

Cream butter and sugar thoroughly. Sift flour, salt and baking soda 3 times. Add small amounts of flour to creamed mixture alternately with milks, beating until smooth after each addition. Add flavoring. Beat egg whites until fluffy and fold in. Grease 3 (9-inch) cake pans lightly flour and line bottom with waxed paper. Bake in preheated 350° oven for 25 to 30 minutes or until cake springs back when tested.

Filling:

8 egg yolks
1 c. sugar
1 c. chopped pecans
½ c. whiskey

2 c. grated coconut
1 c. white raisins
1 stick butter, softened

Beat egg yolks until light. Gradually add sugar and softened butter and beat well. Cook in top of double boiler until slightly thickened, stirring constantly. While the above is being prepared combine nuts, coconut, raisins and whiskey and let soak. Fold into thickened mixture. Alternate layers of cake and filling. After assembling cake in layers it may be iced with white icing.

Joan Johnson

Mandarin Orange Cake

1 yellow buttery cake mix
3 eggs

½ c. oil
1 can mandarin oranges, drained

Mix these ingredients together and pour into 3 prepared cake pans. Bake until done. **Filling:** Mix container of Cool Whip, 1 (3.4-ounce)

(continued)

vanilla instant pudding and 1 small can pineapple. Spread onto the 3 layers. Keep refrigerated.

Joan Johnson

Buttermilk Pound Cake

6 eggs
1 c. Crisco shortening
¼ tsp. salt
3 c. sugar

Baker's Joy
3 c. cake flour
1½ tsp. vanilla
1 c. buttermilk

Spray tube pan with Baker's Joy. Cream together 1 cup Crisco shortening and add 3 cups sugar. Add 6 eggs one at a time and add vanilla. Mix 3 cups cake flour and salt separately. Add the flour mixture into the creamy mixture alternating with 1 cup buttermilk. Pour into tube pan and bake for 1 hour and 15 minutes at 325° until golden brown.

Joan Johnson

Confectioner Sugar Pound Cake

3 sticks butter, softened
Baker's Joy
6 eggs
1 (8-oz.) pkg. cream cheese
1 box sifted confectioners' sugar

1 T. vanilla
⅓ c. evaporated milk
¼ tsp. salt
3 c. all-purpose flour

Spray tube pan with Baker's Joy. Mix 3 sticks softened butter with 6 eggs one at a time. Add 1 (8-ounce) package cream cheese, 1 tablespoon vanilla and 1 box sifted confectioners' sugar to mixture. Add 3 cups sifted all-purpose flour with ¼ teaspoon salt alternating with ⅓ cup evaporated milk. Bake for 1½ hours or until golden brown at 350°.

Joan Johnson

Georgia Pound Cake

½ lb. butter
½ c. Crisco shortening
2½ c. sugar
4 eggs
2 tsp. vanilla

1 c. milk
3 c. all-purpose flour
½ tsp. baking powder
¼ tsp. salt

Cream butter, sugar and shortening together. Add 4 eggs one at a time. Then add 3 cups sifted all-purpose flour, ½ teaspoon baking

(continued)

powder, ¼ teaspoon salt, 2 teaspoons vanilla alternating with 1 cup milk. Pour into greased and floured pan and bake at 325° or until golden brown.

Joan Johnson

OLD-STYLE POUND CAKE

2 c. sifted flour
½ tsp. baking powder
¼ tsp. slat
2 tsp. lemon extract

1 c. margarine or butter
1½ c. sugar
5 eggs

Grease and lightly flour bottom of pan. Cream butter and gradually add sugar, beating well all the time. Beat in eggs one at a time. Add flour, baking powder, salt and lemon extract. Pour into greased pan and bake for 1 hour and 10 minutes at 325°.

Joan Johnson

ORANGE CARROT CAKE

1¼ c. oil
1 c. packed brown sugar
1 c. granulated sugar
4 lg. eggs
2 c. all-purpose flour
Grated zest of 1 fresh orange

1 tsp. baking powder
1 tsp. soda
1 tsp. salt
1 tsp. cinnamon
3 c. shredded carrots
1 tsp. orange extract

Beat oil and sugars well, add eggs one at a time, beating well after each addition. Whisk flour, baking powder, soda, salt and cinnamon. Blend gradually into sugar mixture. Stir in carrots, zest and extract. Divide batter among 3 prepared cake pans. Bake at 325° for 35 minutes or until done. Cool.

Creamy Orange Frosting:

Beat 12 ounces cream cheese, ¾ cup softened margarine, grated zest of fresh orange until smooth. Gradually add 6 cups confectioners' sugar beating until smooth. Blend in 1 teaspoon orange extract. Spread on tops of layers and down sides of cake.

Joan Johnson

PEAR NECTAR-CHERRY DELIGHT CAKE

1 Duncan Hines cherry cake mix
1 sm. pkg. cherry Jello
1 c. Del Monte pear nectar
2/3 c. oil
4 eggs
8 cherries

Grease and flour tube pan. Mix cake mix, dry Jello, pear nectar and oil in a bowl; beat for 2 minutes on medium speed. Add eggs one at a time while beating. Pour into pan and bake for 1 hour at 325°.

Glaze:

1 c. confectioners' sugar mixed with 2-3 T. cherry juice
8 cherries, chopped up

Drizzle over warm cake.

Joan Johnson

PUMPKIN CAKE WITH CREAM CHEESE FROSTING

2 c. all-purpose flour
1 1/2 c. sugar
1 1/4 c. oil
3 1/2 tsp. ground cinnamon
2 tsp. baking soda
2 tsp. baking powder
1 tsp. salt
4 eggs
1 (16-oz.) can pumpkin
1 c. chopped walnuts

Mix oil and sugar together, add eggs one at a time. Mix well. Add pumpkin. Sift flour and spices add to cream mixture. Stir in walnuts. Pour into a greased and floured tube pan and bake for 1 hour at 350°.

Cream Cheese Frosting:

2 (3-oz.) pkgs. cream cheese, softened
1 tsp. vanilla
2 c. confectioners' sugar
2-3 tsp. milk
Dash of salt

Beat with mixer until creamy. Spread over cake.

Joan Johnson

Rum Cake and Sauce

1 (3-oz.) pkg. instant vanilla pudding
1 c. pecans, chopped
4 eggs
½ c. water
½ c. rum
½ c. oil
1 (18-oz.) Duncan Hines butter golden brown cake mix

Grease bundt pan with margarine, spread with pecans. Mix remaining ingredients for cake and mix on medium speed for 2 minutes. Pour into pan and bake at 325° for 50-60 minutes.

Sauce:

1 c. sugar
1 stick margarine
¼ c. water
¼ c. rum

About 10 minutes before cake is done boil ingredients for sauce for 2-3 minutes. When cake is done leave in pan. Prick cake and pour sauce over hot cake in pan. Let cool for 30 minutes. Stores well in refrigerator.

Connie Cullers

Sour Cream Pound Cake

1 c. butter
3 c. sugar
6 eggs
1 (8-oz.) ctn. sour cream
¼ tsp. baking soda
1 tsp. almond extract
½ tsp. vanilla
3 c. sifted all-purpose flour

Cream butter at high speed. Slowly add sugar; beat well. Add eggs one at a time, beating well after each one. Add half of flour and soda, beat well. Add sour cream. Add remaining flour and soda. Add almond extract and vanilla and beat well. Pour into large tube pan and bake at 325° for 2 hours. Spray tube pan with Baker's Joy ahead of time.

Joan Johnson

STRAWBERRY CARROT CAKE

2½ c. all-purpose flour
1¼ c. packed brown sugar
1 c. finely shredded carrots
½ c. oil
½ c. low-fat plain yogurt
1 c. finely chopped strawberries
2 tsp. baking powder
1 tsp. ground cinnamon
½ c. chopped pecans
1 tsp. nutmeg
½ tsp. baking soda
½ tsp. salt
4 eggs
⅓ c. water
Strawberry Cream Cheese Glaze
 (recipe below)

Grease and flour bundt or tube cake pan. Combine all ingredients except strawberries and glaze in a large bowl and beat on low speed for 1 minute. Beat for 2 minutes on medium speed. Fold in strawberries. Pour batter in pan and bake for 45 to 55 minutes at 350°. Cool, remove from pan. Prepare glaze and spoon over top of cake. Refrigerate leftover cake.

Strawberry Cream Cheese Glaze:

Beat 2 ounces cream cheese, softened. Add 1 tablespoon mashed strawberries and ½ teaspoon vanilla in a small bowl on low speed until blended. Gradually beat in ¾ cup powdered sugar until well blended.

Joan Johnson

STRAWBERRY SHORTCUT CAKE

1 c. mini marshmallows
1 pkg. strawberry-flavored gelatin
1½ c. sugar
2 tsp. baking powder
1 c. milk
2 c. sliced strawberries in syrup
1 tsp. vanilla
½ c. shortening
2¼ c. all-purpose flour
½ tsp. salt
3 eggs

Generously grease bottom only of 9 x 13-inch baking pan. Sprinkle marshmallows over bottom. Thoroughly combine thawed strawberries and syrup and dry gelatin; set aside. In a large bowl combine remaining ingredients. Blend at low speed. Pour batter evenly over marshmallows in prepared pan. Spoon strawberry mixture evenly over batter. Bake at 350° for 40-45 minutes. Cut in squares when cool; serve with Cool Whip on top.

Joan Johnson

7-UP CAKE

1 box lemon cake mix
½ c. oil
1 box lemon instant pudding
4 eggs
1 (12-oz.) can 7-Up

Mix all ingredients together. Pour into 3 round, greased and floured cake pans. Bake according to cake mix directions.

Filling:

1 lg. can crushed pineapple
1 c. coconut
1 c. pecans
1 c. sugar
½ c. plain flour
2 eggs

Blend flour and sugar together and add pineapple and eggs. Bring to boil over low heat. Cook until thick and add coconut and pecans.

Joan Johnson

A FAVORITE 4-LAYER DESSERT

Mix together:

1 c. flour
½ c. butter
1 c. finely chopped nuts

Press on bottom of 9 x 11-inch pan. Bake at 350° for 15-20 minutes. Set to cool. Mix:

1 (8-oz.) pkg. cream cheese
1 c. confectioners' sugar
½ (9-oz.) ctn. whipped topping

Spread on cooled crust and chill. Mix:

1 lg. pkg. vanilla or chocolate instant pudding
3 c. milk

Add:

½ tsp. vanilla

Beat until smooth. Pour on cream cheese layer. Top with remaining whipped topping. Sprinkle finely chopped nuts on top or if using chocolate pudding top with milk chocolate bar shavings.

Patsy Pomeroy

Banana Cream Pie

1 (9-inch) baked pastry shell
3 T. cornstarch
1 2/3 c. water
1 (14-oz.) can sweetened condensed milk
3 egg yolks, beaten
2 T. margarine or butter
1 tsp. vanilla
3 med. bananas
ReaLemon lemon juice from concentrate
Whipped cream or whipped topping

In a heavy saucepan dissolve cornstarch in water; stir in condensed milk and egg yolks. Cook and stir until thickened and bubbly. Remove from heat; add margarine and vanilla. Cool slightly. Slice 2 bananas; dip in ReaLemon juice and drain. Arrange on bottom of pastry shell. Pour filling over bananas; cover. Chill for 4 hours or until set. Spread top with whipped cream. Slice remaining banana; dip in ReaLemon juice; drain and garnish top of pie. Refrigerate.

Joan Johnson

Mother's Banana Pudding

1/2 c. sugar
3 T. all-purpose flour
Dash of salt
4 eggs
2 c. milk
1/2 tsp. vanilla extract
1 box vanilla wafers
5-6 med. bananas

Reserve 2 tablespoons sugar. In top of double boiler combine remaining sugar, flour and salt. Beat in 1 whole egg and 3 egg yolks. Reserve egg whites. Stir in milk. Cook uncovered over boiling water, stirring constantly for about 10 minutes or until thickened. Remove from heat and add vanilla. Line bottom and sides of baking dish with vanilla wafers. Slice bananas to cover bottom. Pour custard mixture next and then continue to layer with wafers, bananas and custard. In a small bowl beat reserved egg whites until stiff but not dry. Gradually add reserved 2 tablespoons sugar and a drop or 2 of vanilla. Beat until mixture forms stiff peaks. Spoon on top of custard, spreading to cover entire surface. Make peaks on top. Bake at 425° for 5 minutes or until surface is lightly browned. Serve warm or chilled. Makes 8 servings.

Patsy Pomeroy

BLACKBERRY PIE

4 c. fresh blackberries
½ c. white sugar
½ c. all-purpose flour
1 recipe pastry for 9-inch double pie crust

¼ c. white sugar
2 T. milk

Combine 3½ cups of blackberries with sugar and flour. Spoon the mixture into an unbaked pie shell. Spread the remaining ½ cup berries on top of the sweetened berries. Cover with the top crust. Seal and crimp the edges. Brush the top crust with milk and sprinkle with ¼ cup of sugar. Bake at 425° for 15 minutes. Reduce the temperature to 375° and bake for 20 to 25 minutes. Good served warm with ice cream.

Patsy Pomeroy

COCONUT CUSTARD PIE

2 c. milk
¾ c. sugar
4 eggs
¼ c. butter or margarine

½ c. biscuit mix
1½ tsp. vanilla
1 c. flaked coconut

Combine milk, sugar, eggs, butter, biscuit mix and vanilla in electric blender. Cover and blend on low speed for 3 minutes. Pour into greased 9-inch pie pan. Let stand for about 5 minutes; then sprinkle with coconut. Bake at 350° for 40 minutes. Serve warm or cold.

Joan Johnson

COCONUT CREAM PIE

¾ c. sugar
⅛ tsp. salt
3 egg yolks
1½ tsp. margarine or butter
3 egg whites
1 pastry shell

¼ c. cornstarch or flour
3 c. milk
¾ c. flaked coconut
1 tsp. vanilla
¼ c. sugar

Combine sugar, salt and cornstarch. Combine milk and egg yolks; gradually stir in sugar mixture. Cook over medium heat stirring constantly until mixture thickens and boils. Boil for 1 minute longer stirring constantly. Remove from heat and stir in ½ cup coconut, butter and vanilla. Immediately pour filling into pre-baked pastry shell. Cover the filling with waxed paper. Beat egg whites at high speed for 1

(continued)

minute. Gradually add ¼ cup sugar, beating until stiff and forms peak. Remove waxed paper and spoon whites over filling sealing to edges of pastry. Sprinkle ¼ cup coconut over meringue. Bake for 12 to 15 minutes or until golden brown at 325°.

Joan Johnson

CHEESECAKE

1 c. graham cracker crumbs
3 T. butter or margarine, melted
1 c. plus 3 T. sugar, divided
5 (8-oz.) pkgs. Philadelphia cream cheese, softened
1 T. vanilla
3 eggs
1 c. sour cream
3 T. flour
1 (21-oz.) can cherry pie filling

Mix crumbs, 3 tablespoons sugar and butter; press into bottom of 9-inch springform pan. Bake at 350° for 10 minutes. Beat cream cheese, 1 cup sugar, flour and vanilla on medium speed until well blended. Add eggs one at a time on low speed. Blend in sour cream. Pour over crust. Bake at 350° for 65 minutes or until center is almost set. Cool before removing rim from pan. Chill for 4 hours or more. Top with pie filling.

Joan Johnson

CHERRY CHEESECAKE

1 (9-inch) graham cracker crumb crust
1 (8-oz.) pkg. cream cheese, softened
1 (14-oz.) can condensed milk
⅓ c. ReaLemon juice
1 tsp. vanilla
1 (21-oz.) can cherry pie filling, chilled

In a medium bowl beat cream cheese until fluffy. Add sweetened milk; blend well. Stir in lemon juice and vanilla. Pour into pie crust and chill for 2 to 3 hours. Top with chilled cherry pie filling.

Joan Johnson

Chocolate Morsel Pie

2 eggs
½ c. sugar
1 c. chopped walnuts
1 c. butter, melted & cooled
1 (6-oz.) pkg. semi-sweet chocolate morsels
½ c. all-purpose flour
1 (9-inch) unbaked pie shell
½ c. firmly packed brown sugar

Preheat oven to 325°. In a large bowl beat eggs until foamy. Add flour, sugar and brown sugar; beat until well blended. Blend in melted butter. Stir in chocolate morsels and walnuts. Pour into pie shell and bake for 1 hour. Let cool and serve with ice cream or whipped cream.

Joan Johnson

Icebox Pie

1 (9-inch) graham cracker crust
1 tsp. vanilla
1 can blueberry or cherry pie filling
5 oz. Cool Whip
⅓ c. lemon juice
½ tsp. almond extract
1 can condensed milk

Blend vanilla, condensed milk, Cool Whip, almond extract and lemon juice. Fold in pie shell and spread some of the pie filling over the top. Refrigerate.

Connie Cullers

Ice Cream Pie and Sauce

1 (9-inch) prepared graham cracker pie shell
½ gal. vanilla ice cream, softened
½ (6-oz.) bag Bits O'Brickle

Spoon half of softened ice cream into prepared pie shell. Sprinkle ½ bag Bits O'Brickle on top. Heap with remaining ice cream. Freeze.

Sauce:

1½ c. sugar
1 c. evaporated milk
Remaining bag Bits O'Brickle
¼ c. butter
Dash of salt
¼ c. light corn syrup

Combine sugar, milk, butter, syrup and salt. Bring to a boil over low heat; boil for 1 minute. Remove from heat and stir in remaining Bits O'Brickle. Cool stirring occasionally. Chill. To serve, stir sauce well

(continued)

and then spoon over individual pie wedges. Remaining sauce may be stored in refrigerator and used as topping sauce. Serves 8.

Patsy Pomeroy

KEY LIME PIE

1¼ c. graham cracker crumbs
¼ c. firmly packed light brown sugar
½ c. butter, melted
2 (14-oz.) cans sweetened condensed milk

Lime slices for garnish
1 c. fresh Key lime juice
2 egg whites
¼ tsp. cream of tartar
2 T. sugar
⅛ tsp. vanilla

Combine graham cracker crumbs, light brown sugar and melted butter. Press into 9-inch pie plate. Bake at 350° for 10 minutes; cool. Stir together milk and lime juice until blended. Pour into crust. Beat egg whites and cream of tartar at high speed with hand mixer until foamy. Add sugar, 1 tablespoon at a time, beating constantly. Add vanilla and continue beating until forms peaks. Spread meringue over filling. Bake at 325° for 25 to 28 minutes. Chill for 8 hours before serving and garnish with lime slices.

Patsy Pomeroy

LEMON ICEBOX PIE

3 eggs
1 can condensed milk
½ c. fresh lemon juice

1 tsp. vanilla
2 T. sugar
1 graham cracker crust shell

Separate 3 eggs reserving egg whites. Beat 3 egg yolks; add 1 can condensed milk, ½ cup of fresh lemon juice and 1 teaspoon vanilla. Pour into pie shell. Beat 3 egg whites until stiff; add 2 tablespoons sugar gradually and beat until forms stiff peaks. Spoon this over top of pie mixture and bake in a 300° oven until whites are golden brown.

Joan Johnson

OATMEAL PIE

⅔ c. regular oats
⅔ c. light corn syrup
2 eggs, beaten
⅔ c. sugar

1 tsp. vanilla
¼ tsp. salt
⅔ c. butter, melted
1 (8-inch) pie shell

(continued)

Mix all ingredients thoroughly. Bake in pie shell for 1 hour at 350°. Cool.

Joan Johnson

PEACH COBBLER

1 stick butter
1 c. sugar
1 c. milk
1 c. fresh peaches, cut up
1 c. self-rising flour

Put butter in baking dish and place in oven to melt. Mix sugar and flour; add milk slowly to prevent lumping. Pour over melted butter. Do not stir. Spoon fruit on top. Do not stir, batter will rise to top during baking. Bake in preheated 350° oven for 45 to 50 minutes. Other fruit may be used with this recipe.

Patsy Pomeroy

EASY DOES IT PEANUT BUTTER PIE

1 c. heavy cream
1 (8-oz.) pkg. cream cheese, softened
1 box Dream Whip
1 c. peanut butter
1 c. powdered sugar
1 chocolate crumb pie crust

Combine peanut butter, softened cream cheese and powdered sugar in a mixing bowl. Blend with mixer until smooth. In a separate bowl beat heavy cream on high until soft peaks form. Gently fold whipped heavy cream into peanut butter mixture. Pour into chocolate crumb crust. Place in refrigerator. Prepare Dream Whip according to package directions using both envelopes. Spread on top of pie. Chill for at least 2 hours.

Patsy Pomeroy

PECAN PIE

3 eggs
1 c. sugar
1 c. dark corn syrup
1/4 tsp. salt
3 T. margarine
2 1/2 tsp. vanilla
1 (9-inch) pie shell
1 c. pecans
Aluminum foil

(continued)

Beat eggs lightly and add corn syrup; mix well. Add sugar, salt and vanilla; mix thoroughly. Let stand for 5 minutes. Melt 3 tablespoons margarine and add to mixture. Pour into pie shell. Add 1 cup whole or chopped pecans over the top. Place foil around edges of crust to prevent it from burning. Bake for 40-45 minutes at 350°.

Joan Johnson

Sweet Potato Pie

1½ c. cooked sweet potatoes or canned
¾ c. sugar
½ tsp. salt
1¼ tsp. cinnamon
1 tsp. ginger
½ tsp. nutmeg
¼-½ tsp. cloves
3 eggs, slightly beaten
⅓-½ c. milk
⅓-½ c. evaporated milk
1 pastry shell

Thoroughly combine all ingredients; pour into pastry shell. Bake for 50 minutes. Cool and serve with Cool Whip. Bake at 350°.

Joan Johnson

Walnut Pumpkin Pie

1 (6-oz.) graham cracker pie crust
1 (15-oz.) can pumpkin
1 (14-oz.) can sweetened condensed milk
1 egg
1¼ tsp. cinnamon
½ tsp. ginger
½ tsp. nutmeg
½ tsp. salt
¼ c. packed brown sugar
2 T. all-purpose flour
2 T. cold margarine or butter
¼ c. chopped walnuts

Preheat oven to 425°. Combine pumpkin, condensed milk, egg, ¼ teaspoon cinnamon, ginger, nutmeg and salt; mix well. Turn into pie shell. Bake for 15 minutes; remove pie. Reduce oven temperature to 350°. In a small bowl combine sugar, flour and remaining ½ teaspoon cinnamon; cut in margarine until crumbly. Stir in walnuts. Sprinkle mixture evenly over pie. Bake for 40 minutes or until done. Cool.

Joan Johnson

Banana Ice Cream

1 c. half & half
2 c. whipping cream
1 (14-oz.) can sweetened
  condensed milk (not evaporated)

2 ripe bananas
2 T. vanilla

In a large bowl combine ingredients. Pour into ice cream freezer. Freeze according to manufacturer's instructions. Freeze leftovers. Can also use strawberries, peaches, etc.

Joan Johnson

Butter Pecan Ice Cream

Sauté:

2 c. chopped pecans

3 T. margarine

Cool. Blend:

1 (14-oz.) can sweetened
  condensed milk
1 tsp. maple flavoring

2 c. (1 pt.) half & half
2 c. (1 pt.) whipping cream

In a large bowl combine sweetened condensed milk, pecans and flavoring; mix well. Stir in remaining ingredients. Pour into ice cream freezer container. Freeze according to directions.

Joan Johnson

Vanilla Ice Cream

2 c. (1 pt.) half & half
2 c. (1 pt.) whipping cream
1 can sweetened condensed milk
  (not evaporated)

2 T. vanilla

In a large bowl combine ingredients; mix well. Pour into ice cream freezer. Freeze according to manufacturer's instructions. Freeze leftovers.

Joan Johnson

Recipe Favorites

Cookies & Candy

Helpful Hints

- Unbaked cookie dough can be covered and refrigerated for up to 24 hours or frozen in an airtight container for up to 9 months.

- Bake one cookie sheet at a time on the middle oven rack.

- Decorate cookies with chocolate by placing cookies on a rack over waxed paper. Dip the tines of a fork into melted chocolate and wave the fork gently back and forth to make line decorations.

- Some cookies need indentations on top to fill with jam or chocolate. Use the rounded end of a honey dipper.

- Dip cookie cutters in flour or powdered sugar and shake off excess before cutting. For chocolate dough, dip cutters in baking cocoa.

- Tin coffee cans make excellent freezer containers for cookies.

- If you only have one cookie sheet on hand, line it with parchment paper. While one batch is baking, load a second sheet of parchment paper to have another batch ready to bake. Cleanup will be easier.

- When a recipe calls for packed brown sugar, fill the correct size measuring cup with sugar and use one cup size smaller to pack the brown sugar into its cup.

- Cut-up dried fruit often sticks to the blade of your knife. To prevent this problem, coat the blade of your knife with a thin film of vegetable spray before cutting.

- Instead of folding nuts into brownie batter, sprinkle on top of batter before baking. This keeps nuts crunchy instead of soggy.

- Only use glass or shiny metal pans. Dark or nonstick pans will cause brownies to become soggy and low in volume.

- When making bars, line pan with aluminum foil and prepare as directed. The bars can be lifted out, and cleanup is easy.

- Cutting bars is easier if you score the bars right as the pan leaves the oven. When the bars cool, cut along the scored lines.

- Use a double boiler for melting chocolate to prevent it from scorching. A slow cooker on the lowest setting also works well for melting chocolate, especially when coating a large amount of candy.

- Parchment paper provides an excellent nonstick surface for candy. Waxed paper should not be used for high-temperature candy.

Cookies & Candy

Brownies

2 c. sugar
1 stick butter
½ c. shortening
1 c. water
¼ c. unsweetened cocoa

2 eggs
½ c. buttermilk
2 c. all-purpose flour
1 tsp. baking soda
1 tsp. vanilla

In a large mixing bowl combine the flour and sugar. In a heavy saucepan combine butter, shortening, water and cocoa. Stir and heat until boiling. Pour boiling mixture over the flour and sugar. Add the buttermilk, eggs, baking soda and vanilla. Mix well with mixer on high speed. Pour into a well buttered 17½ x 11-inch pan. Bake at 400° for 20 minutes or until tests done in center.

Frosting:

½ c. butter
2 T. dark cocoa

3½ c. unsifted powdered sugar
1 tsp. vanilla

In a saucepan combine the butter, cocoa and milk. Heat to boiling stirring constantly. Mix in powdered sugar and vanilla until frosting is smooth. Pour warm frosting over brownies as soon as you take them out of oven. Cool. Cut into 48 brownies.

Joan Johnson

Blonde Brownies

2 c. margarine
2 c. brown sugar
2 tsp. vanilla
2 eggs

2 c. self-rising flour
½ c. chocolate chips
½ c. chopped pecans

Melt the 2 cups margarine and add 2 cups brown sugar. Mix until creamy then add 2 teaspoons vanilla and 2 slightly beaten eggs. Fold in 2 cups self-rising flour gradually. Pour mixture into lightly greased and floured oblong dish. Spread ½ cup chocolate chips and ½ cup

(continued)

chopped pecans over the top and press into mixture. Bake at 350° until lightly golden brown.

Joan Johnson

Fudge Brownies

4 c. sugar
8 eggs
1¼ c. butter
2 c. all-purpose flour

1¼ c. cocoa
2 tsp. vanilla
1 tsp. salt
2 c. chopped walnuts

Cream butter and sugar in a bowl. Combine flour, cocoa and salt; add to creamed mixture and mix well. Stir in vanilla and walnuts. Spread into greased 15 x 10 x 1-inch baking pan. Bake at 325° for 40-45 minutes or until brownies test done. Cool for 10 minutes.

Frosting:

½ c. butter
1½ squares unsweetened chocolate
3 c. confectioners' sugar

5 T. milk
1 tsp. vanilla
Chopped walnuts

Melt the butter and chocolate. Place in a mixing bowl. Add half of the confectioners' sugar; mix well. Add milk, vanilla and remaining sugar and beat until smooth. Spread immediately over warm brownies. Sprinkle with nuts. Makes 3 dozen.

Joan Johnson

Butter Almond Crescent Cookies

1 c. butter, softened
1 c. confectioners' sugar, divided
1 c. finely chopped almonds

2 c. all-purpose flour
1 tsp. almond extract

In a large bowl beat butter with ½ cup sugar until light and fluffy. Blend in almond extract. Sift flour and gradually add to mixture along with almonds. Blend together until it forms dough. Shape dough into a ball, seal in plastic wrap and refrigerate for at least 1 hour. Divide dough into 8 pieces. Flour hands and work surface. Shape each piece into a ½-inch thick roll. Cut each roll in 2-inch pieces. Arrange on ungreased cookie sheets and shape each into crescent tapering the ends by gently pinching them. Bake in a preheated oven at 350° for 18-20

(continued)

minutes or until faintly brown. Cool completely, dust tops with remaining sifted confectioners' sugar. Makes 3 dozen cookies.

Joan Johnson

BUTTERSCOTCH BABBLES

2 (12-oz.) pkgs. butterscotch chips
1 c. miniature marshmallows
2 c. Rice Krispies
8 oz. peanuts
½ c. peanut butter

Place butterscotch chips and peanut butter in saucepan and melt. Add peanuts and Rice Krispies and blend well. Add marshmallows and stir slightly. Drop onto wax paper. Freeze.

Patsy Pomeroy

CHOCOLATE COW PIES

2 c. (12 oz.) milk chocolate chips
1 T. shortening
½ c. raisins
½ c. chopped, slivered almonds

In a double boiler over simmering water melt the chocolate chips and shortening stirring until smooth. Remove from the heat; stir in raisins and almonds. Drop by tablespoons onto waxed paper. Chill until ready to serve.

Joan Johnson

CHOCOLATE CRINKLE COOKIES

2 c. granulated sugar
½ c. margarine
2 tsp. vanilla
4 eggs
4 oz. unsweetened chocolate
2 tsp. baking powder
2 c. all-purpose flour
½ tsp. salt
1 c. confectioners' sugar
Wax paper

Mix together 2 cups granulated sugar, ½ cup margarine, 2 teaspoons vanilla and 4 eggs. Melt 4 ounces unsweetened chocolate then cool. Mix in cooled chocolate. Stir in 2 cups all-purpose flour, 2 teaspoons baking powder and ½ teaspoon salt slowly. Refrigerate dough for at least 2 hours. Drop dough by teaspoon onto 1 cup confectioners' sugar which was sprinkled on wax paper. Roll and shape into balls. Place 2 inches apart on greased baking sheet. Bake for 12-14 minutes at 350°.

Joan Johnson

No-Bake Chocolate Oatmeal Cookies

1 stick butter
2 c. sugar
¼ c. cocoa
½ c. milk
¼ c. chunky peanut butter
1 tsp. vanilla
Wax paper
3 c. quick-cooking oatmeal

Mix together in a heavy saucepan 1 stick butter, 2 cups sugar, ½ cup cocoa and ½ cup milk. Stir and let come to boil. Boil for 1 minute. Remove from heat. Add ¼ cup chunky peanut butter and 1 teaspoon vanilla. Add 3 cups of quick-cooking oatmeal. Stir this real well and then drop by teaspoon onto wax paper.

Joan Johnson

Chess Cake Squares

1 box yellow cake mix
4 eggs
1 box confectioners' sugar
1 stick butter, melted
1 (8-oz.) pkg. cream cheese, softened

Beat mix, butter and one egg together. Press into a 9 x 13-inch greased pan. Mix cream cheese, 3 eggs and sugar together. Pour over crust. Bake at 350° for 35 minutes.

Patsy Pomeroy

Delicious Cinnamon Roll-Ups

8 oz. cream cheese
½ c. sugar
1 tsp. vanilla
1 egg yolk

Blend all together.

1 stick butter, melted
1 T. cinnamon sugar

Take a very fresh loaf of white bread. Trim crust and flatten with a rolling pin. Spread cheese mixture on bread and roll up. Dip in melted butter and cinnamon sugar. Bake for 15 minutes at 350°.

Patsy Pomeroy

Easy Cracker Treat

1 pkg. Club crackers
2 sticks butter
1 c. brown sugar
1 c. pecans, chopped

(continued)

Heat butter and sugar until melted. Add chopped pecans. Dip crackers in mixture and place on wax paper-lined cookie sheet. Bake at 325° for about 10 minutes.

Patsy Pomeroy

CRACKER SNACK

1 pkg. semi-sweet chocolate melting squares
2 sleeves Ritz crackers
Peanut butter

Melt chocolate. Spread peanut butter between crackers and dip in chocolate. Place on wax paper and let chocolate set.

Patsy Pomeroy

FUDGE

3 c. sugar
1 c. milk
1 (7-oz.) jar marshmallow creme
1 c. chopped pecans
1 tsp. vanilla
¾ stick margarine
1 (12-oz.) pkg. chocolate chips

Mix sugar, milk and margarine together. Cook until boils, stirring constantly. Boil for 5 minutes. Remove from heat. Stir in chips and marshmallow creme; stir until creamy smooth. Pour into buttered pan. When set cut in squares.

Joan Johnson

CHOCOLATE-PEANUT BUTTER FUDGE

2½ c. sugar
¼ c. cocoa
1 c. milk
1 T. light corn syrup
½ c. butter, divided
½ c. peanut butter
1 c. chopped pecans
2 tsp. vanilla

Combine first 4 ingredients in a large heavy saucepan. Cook over medium heat stirring constantly until sugar dissolves. Add 2 tablespoons butter and stir until melted. Cover and boil for 3 minutes. Remove cover, continue to cook without stirring until mixture reaches soft ball stage (232°). Remove from heat and add remaining butter, peanut butter, pecans and vanilla (do not stir). Cool for 10 minutes.

(continued)

Cocoa Fudge

2½ c. sugar
1 c. can cream
1½ T. white Karo syrup
1 c. chopped pecans

¼ c. cocoa
½ c. margarine
Dash of salt
2 tsp. vanilla

Cook over medium heat until forms a soft ball in cold water. Take off heat; place pan in cold water. Add vanilla and nuts. Leave in cold water for 3 to 4 minutes then beat until thick. Pour into a buttered pan. When set cut into squares.

Joan Johnson

Date Pecan Roll

3 c. sugar
1 c. milk
6 cherries, chopped

1 pkg. dates, chopped
2 T. butter
1 c. chopped pecans

Mix sugar and milk; bring to a boiling point. Add cherries and dates. Boil slowly until small amount of mixture forms soft ball when dropped in cold water. Remove from heat; add butter, set in a pan of cold water. When lukewarm beat until thick; add nuts. Pour into dampened cloth and shape into a long roll. Chill and slice when cold.

Joan Johnson

Mother's Date Nut Roll

3 c. sugar
1 c. cream or Pet milk
1 (8-oz.) pkg. dates, chopped

¼ stick butter
1 tsp. vanilla
1½ c. chopped pecans

Combine sugar, cream and dates. Boil slowly until soft ball is formed in water. Add butter and vanilla. Mix well. Add chopped pecans and beat until cool. Roll cool mixture in wax paper to make a log. Roll again in damp dish cloth. Let mellow in refrigerator. Slice and serve.

Patsy Pomeroy

DIVINITY

2 c. sugar
½ c. water
½ c. white Karo syrup
Dash of salt

1 tsp. vanilla
2 stiff egg whites
1 c. chopped pecans

In a heavy saucepan combine sugar, water, Karo syrup and salt. Cook and stir until syrup comes to a rapid boil; lower heat to medium. Do not stir any longer but test syrup in cup of cool water every now and again for a hard ball. Then spoon a small amount of syrup, hold it up over the pan to see if a very long string hangs and swings back and forth. Then remove from heat. Add vanilla. Beat egg whites until stiff and then begin pouring syrup into whites beating with mixer. Beat until it begins to lose some gloss and it is thickened some. Add nuts and stir in to push off the spoon. If divinity becomes too stiff while spooning add few drops of hot water.

Joan Johnson

ENGLISH TOFFEE

2 c. sugar
⅔ c. butter
2 T. water
1 (6-oz.) pkg. semi-sweet
 chocolate morsels

1 T. light corn syrup
1 tsp. vanilla
1 c. finely chopped pecans or
 walnuts

Combine sugar, butter, water and corn syrup in 3-quart Dutch oven. Cook over low heat stirring gently until sugar dissolves. Cover and cook over medium heat for 2-3 minutes to wash sugar crystal from sides of pan. Uncover and cook to hard crack stage (300°). Remove from heat and stir in vanilla. Pour into ungreased 15 x 10 x 1-inch jelly-roll pan. Spread to edges of pan. Sprinkle chocolate morsels over toffee; let stand for 1 minute or until chocolate begins to melt. Spread chocolate over entire candy layer; sprinkle with pecans or walnuts. Let stand until set. Break into pieces. Store in airtight container in refrigerator.

Patsy Pomeroy

FRUIT CAKE COOKIES

1 c. brown sugar
¼ c. butter
½ c. wine
2 eggs
½ lb. mixed cherries
½ lb. pineapple
½ tsp. allspice
1½ heaping c. flour
½ tsp. nutmeg
½ tsp. cloves
½ tsp. cinnamon
1 lb. chopped pecans
1 lb. raisins
2 tsp. soda
1½ T. milk

Cream butter and sugar; add wine and eggs. Add gradually one half of the flour. Use rest of flour on fruit mixture. Add the spices. Mix all together; add soda dissolved in milk and mix in. Drop from spoon onto cookie sheet. Put pan of water under cookie sheet. Bake cookies for 30 to 40 minutes at 300°.

Joan Johnson

JELLY TOTS COOKIES

2 c. sifted all-purpose flour
½ tsp. baking powder
¼ tsp. salt
1 c. butter or margarine, softened
1 egg yolk
½ c. sugar
2 T. water
1 tsp. vanilla
1¼ c. finely chopped pecans

Cream butter, egg yolk and sugar in bowl for 1½ minutes. Add water, vanilla and half of flour, baking powder and salt mixed together. Blend very well then add remaining flour mixture Beat for ½ minute. Form dough into balls the size of a small walnut and roll into chopped nuts. Place on lightly greased cookie sheet and bake for 5 minutes at 350°, remove from oven and make an impression in top of each with small thimble. Return to oven, bake for 8 to 10 minutes longer. Remove and add favorite jelly in center. Cool.

Joan Johnson

LEMON SQUARES

2 sticks butter
2 c. flour
½ c. powdered sugar

Mix these together and press into long pan. Bake for 15 minutes at 325°.

(continued)

4 eggs, lightly beaten
2 c. sugar
6 T. lemon juice
Dash of salt
½ baking powder
1 T. flour

Mix these ingredients together and pour over pastry. Bake at 325° for 30 minutes. When slightly cool sprinkle with powdered sugar. Cut in squares when cool.

Joan Johnson

LEMONY CHEESECAKE SQUARES

2 c. vanilla wafer crumbs
¼ c. sugar
½ c. margarine or butter, melted
3 (8-oz.) pkgs. cream cheese, softened
1 (14-oz.) can sweetened condensed milk
3 eggs
½ c. lemon juice from concentrate
¾ c. strawberry preserves

Combine crumbs, sugar and margarine; press firmly on bottom of 9 x 13-inch baking pan. Bake for 8 minutes at 375°. Cool. Reduce oven temperature to 300°. In a large mixing bowl beat cheese until fluffy. Gradually beat in condensed milk until smooth. Add eggs and lemon juice, mix well. Spread preserves evenly over prepared crust. Pour cheese mixture over preserves. Bake for 45 to 50 minutes or until center is set. Cool. Chill thoroughly. Refrigerate leftovers.

Joan Johnson

CHOCOLATE CHIP MERINGUE COOKIES

2 lg. egg whites
½ c. sugar
1 tsp. vanilla
3 T. unsweetened cocoa powder
½ c. semi-sweet chocolate chips

In a large mixing bowl beat egg whites on high speed of electric mixer until they hold stiff peaks. Beat in sugar 1 tablespoon at a time. Add vanilla. Reduce speed to low and beat in cocoa powder. Gently fold in chocolate chips with a rubber spatula. Drop mixture by rounded teaspoonfuls onto foil or parchment-lined baking sheets. Bake at 250° for 1 hour. Turn off oven and leave cookies in oven for about 2 hours longer. Remove from pan; store in airtight container.

Patsy Pomeroy

Oatmeal Drop Cookies

1½ c. sifted all-purpose flour
1 tsp. soda
1 tsp. salt
3 c. quick-cooking oats
1 c. oil, butter or margarine
1 c. firmly packed brown sugar
1 c. raisins

⅓ c. buttermilk
1½ tsp. cinnamon
1½ tsp. vanilla
1 c. sugar
2 eggs
¾ c. chopped nuts

Combine butter, sugars, eggs and vanilla in a large bowl. Cream for 2 minutes. Add flour, soda, salt, cinnamon and oats alternating with the buttermilk. Mix well. Stir in raisins and nuts. Drop by teaspoon onto greased cookie sheet and bake until light brown at 350°.

Joan Johnson

Oatmeal Fudge Bars

2 c. packed brown sugar
2 tsp. vanilla
2½ c. Bisquick baking mix
3 c. quick-cooking oats
1 (12-oz.) pkg. semi-sweet chocolate chips
1 c. chopped nuts

2 eggs
¾ c. margarine, softened
2 T. margarine
½ tsp. salt
1 c. condensed milk
2 tsp. vanilla

Heat oven to 350°. Grease a 15½ x 10½ x 1-inch pan. Mix brown sugar, ¾ cup margarine, eggs and vanilla. Stir in baking mix and oats until uniform consistency. Heat chocolate chips, milk, 2 tablespoons margarine and salt in a 2-quart saucepan over low heat stirring constantly until smooth. Stir in nuts and vanilla. Press about ⅔ of oatmeal mixture with greased hands in pan. Spread chocolate mixture over oatmeal layer. Drop remaining oatmeal mixture by tablespoons onto top. Bake until light brown, about 30 minutes. Cut in bars. Makes 70 bars.

Joan Johnson

Peanut Butter Cookies

1 c. oil
1 c. packed brown sugar
1 tsp. vanilla
2 tsp. soda
1 c. sugar

2 eggs
1 c. peanut butter
½ tsp. salt
3 c. sifted all-purpose flour

(continued)

Cream oil, sugars, eggs and vanilla. Stir in peanut butter. Sift dry ingredients; stir into cream mixture. Drop by teaspoon onto ungreased cookie sheet. Press with the back of a fork to make a criss cross. Bake in a 350° oven for 10 minutes. Makes 5 dozen.

Joan Johnson

PEANUT BUTTER MIDDLES

In a large bowl beat until light and fluffy:

½ c. granulated sugar
½ c. packed brown sugar
¼ c. creamy peanut butter
½ c. margarine, softened

Add:

1 tsp. vanilla
1 egg

Beat well. Stir in until blended:

1½ c. all-purpose flour
½ c. unsweetened cocoa
½ tsp. baking soda

Set aside. In a small bowl combine filling ingredients:

¾ c. peanut butter
¾ c. confectioners' sugar

Blend well. Roll into 30 balls. For each cookie with floured hand shape about 1 tablespoon dough around 1 peanut butter ball covering completely. Place 2 inches apart on ungreased cookie sheet. Flatten with bottom of glass dipped in sugar. Bake in a 375° oven for 7 to 9 minutes or until set and slightly cracked. Cool. Makes 30 cookies.

Joan Johnson

PEANUT BUTTER TEA CAKES

1 pkg. peanut butter cookie dough roll
1 pkg. Reese's chocolate peanut butter cups

Spray Baker's Joy into mini muffin pan cups. Spoon ½ teaspoon cookie dough into each cup. Bake in oven as directed on cookie package. When lightly brown remove from oven. Immediately press a Reese's cup into the middle of each cookie cup. Let cool in pan half a day or overnight. Run a knife around each tea cake if needed then remove.

Joan Johnson

Pecan Balls

1 c. ground pecans
¼ lb. butter
2 T. sugar

1 tsp. vanilla
1 c. flour
Powdered sugar

Mix sugar with butter and vanilla. Add nuts and flour. Form into balls and place on cookie sheet. Bake for 15 minutes or so. Roll in powdered sugar while warm then roll in sugar again. Can increase this recipe if desired. Bake at 350°.

Joan Johnson

Pecan Pie Cookies

1 c. butter
½ c. sugar
½ c. dark corn syrup

2 eggs, separated
2½ c. unsifted all-purpose flour

Filling:

Add:

½ c. confectioners' sugar
¼ c. butter

3 T. dark corn syrup
½ c. finely chopped pecans

Combine, cook over medium heat, stirring occasionally until reaches full boil. Remove and cool. Stir in pecans. **For the cookies:** Cream butter and sugar on low speed for 1 minute. Add corn syrup and egg yolks; beat thoroughly. Chill for a few hours. Beat egg whites slightly. Using 1 tablespoon for each cookie roll into balls, brush lightly with egg whites. Place on greased cookie sheet. Bake at 375° for 5 minutes and then remove from the oven. Roll ½ teaspoon of chilled filling into ball. Firmly press into center of cookie. Return to oven, bake for 5 minutes longer or until lightly browned. Cool.

Joan Johnson

Pecan Pie Bars

Cookie Crust:

Preheat oven to 350°. Spray 15 x 10 x 1-inch baking pan with corn oil cooking spray. In a large bowl with mixer at medium speed beat:

2½ c. flour
1 c. cold butter

½ c. sugar
½ tsp. salt

(continued)

Mix until mixture resembles fine crumbs; press firmly into prepared pan. Bake for 20-23 minutes or until golden brown. Top with filling; finish baking.

4 eggs
1½ c. light or dark corn syrup
1½ tsp. vanilla

3 T. butter or margarine
1½ c. sugar
2½ c. chopped pecans

In a large bowl beat eggs, corn syrup, sugar, butter and vanilla until well blended. Stir in pecans. Immediately pour over hot crust; spread evenly. Bake for 25 minutes or until firm around edges and slightly firm in center. Cool completely. Cut into 2 x 1½-inch bars. Makes about 48 bars.

Joan Johnson

PEOPLE CHOW

1 box Crispix cereal
1 (12-oz.) bag semi-sweet chocolate chips

1 c. peanut butter
1 stick butter
1 box powdered sugar

Pour Crispix into very large bowl that has a secure lid. Melt chocolate chips. Add peanut butter and stick of butter and heat until blended. Pour this mixture over cereal and combine. Add powdered sugar. Put lid on bowl and shake until sugar coated and separated.

Patsy Pomeroy

PEPPERMINT COOKIES

1 (9-oz.) box Famous chocolate wafers
1 (16-oz.) bag York peppermint patties

Sprinkles or candies for decorations (opt.)

Place wafers on microwave-safe plate. Put one peppermint patty on each wafer. Microwave for 15 seconds. Remove from microwave and press another wafer down on top of the cookie with the melting mint. Yields 40 cookies.

Patsy Pomeroy

POTATO CHIP COOKIES

1 c. sugar
1 c. butter (no substitute)
1 egg yolk
1½ c. regular flour

1 c. chopped pecans or walnuts
1 c. crushed potato chips (crushed in your hand)

Cream butter and sugar. Beat in egg yolk, then flour, nuts and crushed chips. Drop by spoonful on ungreased cookie sheet. Bake at 350° for 9 to 10 minutes. Let cool partially before removing. Do not overbake. They will be light in color.

Patsy Pomeroy

PRALINES

1½ c. packed brown sugar
1 c. milk
1 tsp. vanilla

1½ c. pecan halves
3 T. dark corn syrup
1½ c. granulated sugar

Butter sides of heavy 3-quart saucepan. In it combine first 4 ingredients. Heat and stir over medium heat until sugar dissolves and mixture comes to a boil. Then cook to soft ball stage stirring occasionally. Cool for 10 minutes and add vanilla and beat for about 2 minutes. Add pecans and beat until mixture loses its gloss. Drop by heaping tablespoons onto waxed paper.

Joan Johnson

CREAMY PRALINES

¾ c. packed brown sugar
¾ c. granulated sugar
½ c. evaporated milk

2 T. butter
½ tsp. vanilla
1 c. salted, toasted pecans

Mix milk and sugar; bring to a boil. Lower heat to medium and cook until forms a ball in cold water. Remove from heat and add butter, vanilla and pecan halves. Beat until mixture loses its gloss. Drop by spoon onto waxed paper.

Joan Johnson

Spicy Pumpkin Bars

4 lg. eggs
1¾ c. sugar
1 c. oil
2 c. (16-oz.) can solid pack pumpkin

2 c. all-purpose flour
2 tsp. baking powder
1 tsp. salt
2 tsp. pumpkin pie spice
1 c. golden raisins

Preheat oven to 325°. In a mixing bowl beat eggs until frothy; add sugar and beat for 2 minutes. Beat the oil. Sift dry ingredients over the raisins and fold dry mixture into the egg mixture. Do not overmix. Pour into a greased and floured 9 x 13-inch pan. Bake in the preheated oven for 35-40 minutes or until done. Cool and cut into 24 squares.

Joan Johnson

Rocky Road Fudge Bars

Base:

½ c. butter or margarine
1 (1-oz.) square unsweetened chocolate, chopped
1 c. all-purpose flour

1 c. sugar
1 tsp. baking powder
1 tsp. vanilla
¾ c. chopped nuts

Filling:

1 (8-oz.) pkg. cream cheese, softened & reserve 2 oz. for frosting
¼ c. butter or margarine, softened
½ c. sugar

2 T. vanilla
1 egg
¼ c. chopped nuts
1 (6-oz.) pkg. chocolate chips

Frosting:

2 c. miniature marshmallows
¼ c. butter or margarine
¼ c. milk
1 (1-oz.) square unsweetened chocolate, chopped & reserved 2 oz. cream cheese

3 c. powdered sugar
1 tsp. vanilla

Grease and flour 9 x 13-inch pan. In a large saucepan over low heat melt ½ cup butter and 1 ounce unsweetened chocolate, stirring constantly until smooth. Lightly spoon flour into measuring cup. Add 1 cup flour and remaining base ingredients; mix well. Spread into prepared pan. In a small bowl combine all filling ingredients except ¼ cup nuts and chocolate chips. Beat for 1 minute at medium speed

(continued)

until smooth and fluffy; stir in nuts. Spread over chocolate mixture; sprinkle evenly with chocolate chips. Bake at 350° for 25-35 minutes or until center is done. Immediately sprinkle marshmallows over top. Return to oven and bake an additional 2 minutes. In a large saucepan over low heat combine 1/4 cup margarine or butter, milk, 1 ounce unsweetened chocolate and reserved 2 ounces cream cheese; stir until well blended. Remove from heat; stir in powdered sugar and 1 teaspoon vanilla until smooth. Immediately pour frosting over marshmallows and lightly swirl with knife to look marbled. Refrigerate until firm; cut into bars.

Joan Johnson

Rocky Road Squares

1 (12-oz.) pkg. chocolate morsels
1 (14-oz.) can condensed milk
2 T. butter or margarine
2 c. dry roasted peanuts
1 (10½-oz.) pkg. miniature
    marshmallows

In top of double boiler over boiling water melt morsels with condensed milk and butter; remove from heat. In a large bowl combine nuts and marshmallows; fold in chocolate mixture. Spread in wax paper-lined 9 x 13-inch pan. Chill for 2 hours or until firm. Cut in squares, remove from pan and peel off wax paper. Cover with plastic wrap and store at room temperature or keep in refrigerator for 1 day.

Joan Johnson

Rum Balls

1/4 c. rum
2 T. corn syrup
1 c. powdered sugar
2 c. vanilla wafers
1 c. nuts
Grated coconut

Mix rum, corn syrup and sugar together. Crush vanilla wafers; add nuts and mix well together. Pinch a small amount of mixture and roll into balls and then dredge in coconut. Store in refrigerator.

Connie Cullers

Snow Flakes

2 lg. egg whites
3/4 c. sugar
1 (6-oz.) pkg. chocolate chips
1 c. chopped pecans
Pinch of salt
1 tsp. vanilla

(continued)

Preheat oven to 350° for 20 minutes. Turn oven off. Beat egg whites until stiff. Add sugar and salt gradually. Fold in chocolate chips, nuts and vanilla. Drop by teaspoon onto well greased cookie sheet. Leave in oven overnight until oven cools.

Joan Johnson

Recipe Favorites

Recipe Favorites

This & That

Helpful Hints

- Never overcook foods that are to be frozen. Foods will finish cooking when reheated. Don't refreeze cooked, thawed foods.

- When freezing foods, label each container with its contents and the date it was put into the freezer. Always use frozen, cooked foods within 1–2 months.

- To avoid teary eyes when cutting onions, cut them under cold running water or briefly place them in the freezer before cutting.

- Fresh lemon juice will remove onion scent from hands.

- To get the most juice out of fresh lemons, bring them to room temperature and roll them under your palm against the kitchen counter before cutting and squeezing.

- Add raw rice to the salt shaker to keep the salt free flowing.

- Transfer jelly and salad dressings to small plastic squeeze bottles – no more messy, sticky jars!

- Ice cubes will help sharpen garbage disposal blades.

- Separate stuck-together glasses by filling the inside glass with cold water and setting both in hot water.

- Clean CorningWare® by filling it with water and dropping in two denture cleaning tablets. Let stand for 30–45 minutes.

- Always spray your grill with nonstick cooking spray before grilling to avoid sticking.

- To make a simple polish for copper bottom cookware, mix equal parts of flour and salt with vinegar to create a paste.

- Purchase a new coffee grinder and mark it "spices." It can be used to grind most spices; however, cinnamon bark, nutmeg, and others must be broken up a little first. Clean the grinder after each use.

- In a large shaker, combine 6 parts salt and 1 part pepper for quick and easy seasoning.

- Save your store-bought bread bags and ties–they make perfect storage bags for homemade bread.

- Next time you need a quick ice pack, grab a bag of frozen peas or other vegetables out of the freezer.

This & That

Garlic Rub

Take one garlic clove and crush. Mix garlic with course rock salt and course black pepper. This is great to rub on steaks and beef.

Patsy Pomeroy

Homemade Mayonnaise

2 c. oil (more or less depending on amount of juice of the lemon)
2 egg yolks
1 scant tsp. salt
Juice of 1 lemon

All ingredients must be the same temperature. It's best to keep all ingredients refrigerated. Beat egg yolks and salt together until thick. Add juice of one lemon. Continue beating. Reduce speed on mixer and ad oil beginning with a very thin stream until oil and egg begin to blend. Keep adding oil slowly until you reach the desired thickness. This is great on sandwiches and served with tomatoes.

Patsy Pomeroy

Carol's Spiced Pecans

In a large mixing bowl mix together:

3/4 c. sugar
3/4 tsp. salt
1 tsp. cinnamon
1 tsp. cloves
1/4 tsp. allspice
1/4 tsp. nutmeg
2 (1-lb.) bags halved pecans

Beat one egg white with 2½ tablespoons of water. Add to spice mixture. Add 1 cup at a time of nuts to above and coat thoroughly. Lift out with a slotted spoon and spread on cookie sheet. This will coat

(continued)

three or four cups of pecans. Bake at 275° for 45 minute stirring 2 or 3 times while baking. Spread on wax paper to cool.

Patsy Pomeroy

PEPPER JELLY

3 lg. green peppers
12 hot peppers
5 lbs. sugar

3 c. cider vinegar
2 bottles Certo

Core peppers. Place peppers in water in blender and blend until liquid. Cook pepper mixture, vinegar and sugar at a hard boil for 4 minutes. Remove from heat and add Certo. Skim. Pour in sterile jars and seal. It is suggested to use rubber gloves. Yield: 12 (14½-pint) jars.

Patsy Pomeroy

SEVEN-MINUTE ICING

2 unbeaten egg whites
2 tsp. light corn syrup or ¼ tsp. cream of tartar
Fresh coconut

Dash of salt
1½ c. sugar
⅓ c. cold water
1 tsp. vanilla

Place all ingredients except vanilla in top of double boiler and beat for 1 minute then place over boiling water and cook; beating constantly. When frosting forms stiff peaks, about 7 minutes, remove from boiling water. Pour into mixing bowl and add vanilla. Beat until spreading consistency. Spread over top of each layer then down the sides. Sprinkle fresh grated coconut all over top and sides of cake.

Joan Johnson

SHRIMP BUTTER

1 (8-oz.) pkg. cream cheese
1 tsp. lemon juice
¼ c. real butter
1 sm. can shrimp

1 sm. onion
Salt
1 T. Worcestershire sauce

Mix all together. Form 2 balls and wrap into wax paper and freeze. Let thaw for 3 hours before serving.

Connie Cullers

STIR-DROP DOUGHNUTS

2 c. sifted all-purpose flour
3 tsp. baking powder
½ tsp. nutmeg
¾ c. milk
Oil for deep or shallow frying

¼ c. sugar
1 tsp. salt
¼ c. oil
1 egg white

Sift dry ingredients together in a bowl. Pour oil and milk into bowl then add with egg white to dry ingredients. Stir with fork until mixed. Drop the batter by teaspoon into heated oil. Do not crowd in pan. Fry until golden; about 3 minutes. Turn once. Drain on paper towels. Makes 2½ dozen.

Joan Johnson

WAFFLES

3½ c. sifted flour
2 T. baking powder
2 T. sugar
1½ tsp. salt

4 eggs
3 c. milk
¾ c. cooking oil

Sift together 3½ cups sifted flour, 2 tablespoons each baking powder and sugar and 1½ teaspoons salt. Beat 4 egg whites until stiff but not dry. Set aside. Beat 4 egg yolks until lemon colored. Continue beating adding 3 cups milk and ¼ cup cooking oil. Add dry ingredients and beat until smooth. Fold in beaten egg whites. Pour 1 cup batter on preheated waffle grid. Close unit and bake.

Joan Johnson

WHITE BARBECUE SAUCE

1½ c. mayonnaise
¼ c. white wine vinegar
1 T. Creole mustard
1 tsp. sugar
2 tsp. prepared horseradish

¼ c. water
1 T. coarsely ground pepper
1 tsp. salt
2 cloves garlic, minced

Whisk together all ingredients until blended. Store in refrigerator for up to 2 weeks.

Patsy Pomeroy

Mandarin Orange Vinaigrette

1 (8-oz.) can mandarin oranges
¼ c. red wine vinegar
¼ tsp. salt
¼ tsp. black pepper
1 T. honey
⅔ c. vegetable oil

Drain oranges and put into blender or food processor. Add the vinegar, salt, pepper and honey. Start blending slowly and add oil slowly in a thin stream until all the oil is thoroughly blended. Serve at once or cover and refrigerate until ready to serve. Shake well before serving. Will stay fresh in refrigerator for up to 2 weeks.

Patsy Pomeroy

Raspberry Vinaigrette

3 T. seedless all-fruit raspberry jam
1 c. vegetable oil
⅓ c. red wine vinegar
¼ tsp. salt
¼ tsp. black pepper

Put the jam in a glass measuring cup and microwave uncovered at high for 15 seconds or just until the jam melts. Add the vinegar, salt and pepper and whisk until well combined. Add the oil slowly in a thin stream whisking constantly until it is thoroughly blended. Serve at once or cover and refrigerate until ready to serve. Mix well before serving. Will stay fresh for up to 2 weeks in refrigerator.

Patsy Pomeroy

Honey-Mustard Dressing

1 c. mayonnaise
2 T. chopped fresh basil
2 T. vegetable oil
½ tsp. minced garlic
3 T. yellow mustard
3 T. honey
2 tsp. cider vinegar
¼ tsp. ground red pepper

Whisk together all ingredients; cover and chill for at least 4 hours. Makes about 1¾ cups.

Patsy Pomeroy

Family Holiday Meals

A Southern Thanksgiving Feast

by Patsy Pomeroy

Select a nice Butterball turkey - (Fresh turkeys are especially nice and you do not have to wait for the defrost time).

Remove giblets and neck from turkey and put aside. Wash and clean turkey inside and out. Sprinkle some salt in your damp hand and rub inside the turkey and on the outside. Do the same with Vegetable Oil.

Place turkey in roaster pan breast side up. Use poultry picks to close tail opening of turkey and tuck legs back under skin. Insert meat thermometer. Bake uncovered until golden brown. Baste real well with butter and place a little butter inside cavity of turkey before closing up. Use a basting tube and continue basting about every hour. Add a little more butter as needed. Bake at 325° until meat thermometer reaches poultry temperature usually about 3 ½ to 4 ½ hours depending on size of turkey. After turkey turns golden brown, place a sheet of aluminum foil on top until temperature is reached.

After turkey is done, place on hotmat and let sit until able to transport to platter and ready to slice. Save broth in pan for dressing recipe, gravy and leftover turkey soup (recipe in cookbook).

Place the giblets (neck, gizzards, liver and heart) in a small pan and cover with water. Add a little salt and let simmer while turkey is baking. You will chop and use this in your dressing and gravy.

Southern Style Dressing

I do not stuff turkey with my dressing. I bake in a baking dish.

I use Aunt Jemima Cornbread Mix recipe and bake according to directions in my cast iron skillet.
2 slices of toasted white bread
¾ c. sauteed chopped onion
¾ c. sauteed chopped celery
2 eggs beaten
½ c. chopped giblets
1 c. of turkey broth from roasting pan and juice from giblets.

Crumble up cornbread and mix with other ingredients and place in baking dish. Add a little more turkey broth and dot with butter. Bake at 350° for approximately 30 minutes or until golden brown on top. I saute onion and celery with butter in small pan inside oven while turkey is roasting. It makes the kitchen smell wonderful! The dressing is wonderful topped with my giblet gravy.

Giblet Gravy

Melt 1 stick of butter in a cast iron skillet. Add 2 Tablespoons flour and let brown lightly. It will look lumpy. Add 1 cup of milk and stir until mixed thoroughly and let simmer for a little while. Add remaining chopped giblets and 1 cup of turkey broth. If you do not have enough giblets, I use a little of the turkey. Mix well and let simmer. Season with salt and pepper if desired. I like to add a sliced boiled egg to my gravy.

Cranberry Sauce

I chill my jellied cranberry sauce and serve sliced with turkey.

Creamed Corn

10 ears of fresh corn. Shuck and clean corn. Cut corn off the cob into a baking dish. Scrape cob for remaining corn milk. Salt and pepper to taste. Mix 1 cup of milk with 2 tablespoons of flour in a dish and add to corn. Dot with butter and bake at 350° for approximately 35 minutes.

Fresh Pole Beans with New Potatoes

Wash beans in water in sink. Pick off ends and snap beans. Place in large pot and cover with water. Peel small new potatoes and add to beans. Salt and pepper to taste. Add a little bacon grease to pot of beans and cook on low for about 3 hours. Add water as needed.

Deviled Eggs

Boil eggs and peel. Remove yolk and place in bowl. Mix yolk with a little mayonnaise and mustard. Add sweet pickle relish and mix together. Add salt and pepper to taste. Restuff egg whites with mixture. Keep covered in refrigerator until ready to serve.

Southern Pecan Pie

1 c. of ½ light and
 ½ dark corn syrup
3 eggs slightly beaten
1 c. of sugar
2 T. of melted butter

dash of salt
1 tsp. vanilla
1 c. of whole pecans
1 unbaked 9-inch deep
 dish pie crust

Mix first 6 ingredients and then mix in pecans. Pour into pie crust. Bake at 350° for 50 - 55 minutes.

Family Christmas Dinner

Patsy Pomeroy

Our family likes a nice baked ham for Christmas. I buy a shoulder ham with bone. It will depend on size of ham as to how long you will bake it. Usually I bake ham for 3 hours and the skin is charred a little on the outside. I peel the skin aside and slice the nice completely baked ham.

I serve the following recipes with the ham:

Pineapple Casserole

1 (20-oz.) can pineapple chunks
½ c. sugar
1 c. sharp cheddar cheese, grated
3 T. all-purpose flour
½ c. butter, melted
1 c. Ritz crackers, crumbled

Drain pineapple and reserve 3 tablespoons of juice. Combine sugar and flour and stir in 3 tablespoons of pineapple juice. Add grated cheese and pineapple chunks. Mix well, spoon into greased 1 quart casserole. Combine butter and Ritz crackers. Sprinkle on top. Bake in oven at 350 degrees for 30 to 35 minutes.

Green Bean Casserole

1 can french style green beans
1 can of onion rings
1 can cream of mushroom soup

Use baking dish and layer each ingredient twice. I put ½ can of green beans, ½ can mushroom soup, ½ can of onion rings, rest of green beans, rest of mushroom soup and reserve onion rings until last 5 minutes of baking time. Pour a little of green bean juice over top and bake at 350 degrees for 30 minutes. Add rest of onion rings and bake an additional 5 minutes.

Spinach Stuffed Tomatoes

8 tomatoes
2 pkgs. chopped spinach
1 c. grated Parmesan
1 c. bread crumbs
3 green onions, chopped

2 eggs
3 T. butter, melted
½ tsp. thyme
¼ tsp. garlic salt
dash of hot sauce

Cut out pulp from tomatoes. Salt and drain. Cook spinach and drain. Mix together spinach with other ingredients. Stuff tomatoes with mixture. Bake at 325 degrees for 30 minutes.

Christmas Ambrosia
(This can be used in place of Pineapple Casserole)

3 fresh oranges peeled
grated coconut
1 can of pineapple chunks

1 small jar maraschino cherries

Cut oranges into chunks discarding seeds. Add pineapple chunks, grated coconut and cherries. Place in dessert cups at each place setting.

Plum Cake

1 c. buttery flavored oil
2 c. sugar
3 eggs
1 tsp. cloves
1 tsp. cinnamon

1 tsp. lemon flavoring
2 sm. jars plum baby food
2 c. self-rising flour
1 c. chopped pecans

Cream oil, sugar and eggs together. Mix all ingredients together. Bake in a greased and floured tube pan at 325 degrees for 1 hour and 15 minutes. While still warm, glaze with melted butter, confectioners sugar and lemon juice.

Fourth of July Barbecue

Patsy Pomeroy

Barbecue Ribs and Chicken

whole fresh fryer cut up
slab of spareribs
salt and pepper to taste
Kraft Original Barbecue Sauce

Cut up fryer and place in electric skillet or large skillet with enough water to cover. Do the same with ribs. Let water come to boil then reduce heat and simmer for about 30 to 40 minutes. (Put leftover chicken broth in container and freeze for homemade soup).

Place chicken and ribs in foil covered shallow pan. Salt and pepper to taste. Baste with barbecue sauce and with tongs place on hot grill. Continue turning and basting until nice and brown.

Baked Beans

2 cans of Bush's Pork and Beans
¼ cup light brown sugar
2 T. Aunt Jemima Maple Syrup
1 T. Kraft's Original Barbecue Sauce
1 slice of bacon

In baking dish add beans, brown sugar, syrup and barbecue sauce. Top with slice of bacon and bake at 350 degrees for 45 minutes.

Cole Slaw

1 med. size green cabbage
1 T. chopped onion
1/8 tsp. lemon juice
3 T. mayonnaise
salt to taste

Slice cabbage in half. Use knife to slice shreds of cabbage into bowl. Add chopped onion and lemon juice. Add mayonnaise gradually and mix well. Add salt to taste.

Sliced Tomatoes

Fresh tomatoes sliced, sprinkle with salt and pour Zesty Italian Dressing over slices, cover and let sit in refrigerator for a while before serving.

Watermelon Fruit Bowl

Cut a watermelon in half and remove pulp and seeds from one of the halves. With sharp knife, scallop edge of watermelon half. Cut up watermelon into small chunks and place back in melon. Add cut up cantaloupe, blueberries, honeydew melon and strawberries.

Homemade Ice Cream

4 eggs
2 ½ c. of sugar
6 c. of milk
4 c. of light cream
2 T. vanilla
½ tsp. salt

Beat eggs until light. Add sugar gradually, beating until mixture thickens. Add remaining ingredients, mix thoroughly. Freeze in ice cream freezer. Makes 1 gallon.

You can add chocolate chips, fresh peaches cut up or one of our favorites is frozen Mint Girl Scout Cookies.

Chocolate Chip Cookie Cake

Take one roll of Pillsbury Slice and Bake Chocolate Chip Cookie Dough and spread and form into a pizza pan. Bake according to directions. On top decorate with red, white and blue frosting. Serve with ice cream.

White Butter Frosting

⅓ c. soft butter
3 c. sifted confectioners sugar
about 3 T. cream
1 ½ tsp. vanilla

Blend butter and sugar thoroughly. Stir in cream and vanilla until smooth. Separate into bowls and add a few drops of food coloring.

INDEX OF RECIPES

APPETIZERS & BEVERAGES

BACON WRAPS	1
BANANA GONE BAD SMOOTHIE	9
BARBEQUE SHRIMP	7
BLONDE SANGRIA	11
BLOODY MARY	9
BOILED SHRIMP	7
CHAMPAGNE PUNCH	10
CHEESE BALL	2
COCKTAIL SAUSAGE IN SAUCE	6
CRABBY CLUB PIZZETTAS	3
CRABMEAT CANAPES	4
DEVILED CRAB	4
FRUIT SLUSH	10
GALA PUNCH	11
GUACAMOLE DIP	5
HOT ARTICHOKE DIP	1
HOT BUTTERED RUM	9
HOT CHIPPED BEEF DIP	3
HOT CIDER PUNCH	11
ITALIAN SQUARES	5
MARINATED SHRIMP	7
MARY'S SASSY SALSA	6
OLIVE CHEESE BALLS	2
ORANGE DRINK	10
PEGGY'S CRAB SPREAD	4
PRALINE-TOPPED BRIE	1
SAUCY CRAB BALL	3
SAUSAGE STUFFED MUSHROOMS	6
SOUTHERN CAVIAR	2
SPICED MOCHA MIX	10
SPINACH DIP	8
SPINACH DIP IN CABBAGE	8
SWEDISH MEATBALLS	5
TACO DIP	8
WASSAIL	11
WINE COOLER	12

SOUPS & SALADS

AMBROSIA MOLD	16
CHEESY WILD RICE SOUP	14
CLASSIC ONION SOUP	13
CONGEALED STRAWBERRY SALAD	19
CREAM OF SPINACH SOUP	15
CUCUMBER SALAD	17
FROZEN CRANBERRY BANANA SALAD	17
FROZEN FRUIT SALAD	18
FRUIT SALAD	18
JOAN'S CHICKEN SOUP	13
JOAN'S CHUNKY FRUIT CHICKEN SALAD	17
JOAN'S CREAMY POTATO SOUP	14
LEFTOVER THANKSGIVING TURKEY SOUP	15
MARINATED BROCCOLI SALAD	16
MARINATED COLESLAW	16
1905 SALAD	20
POTATO AND GROUND BEEF SOUP	13
SHRIMP OR LOBSTER BISQUE	15
STRAWBERRY JELLO SALAD	19
STRAWBERRY PRETZEL SALAD	19
WEST INDIES SALAD	20

VEGETABLES & SIDE DISHES

AU GRATIN POTATOES	26
BUTTERY CINNAMON SKILLET APPLES	23
CABBAGE CASSEROLE	23
CAULIFLOWER CASSEROLE	24
CHEESY POTATOES	27
COOKED SQUASH AND TOMATOES	29
CRAB STUFFED POTATOES	27
FRESH COLLARD GREENS	24
FRIED GREEN TOMATOES	31
FRIED OKRA	25
GARLIC GRITS	25
GREEN PEPPER POTATOES	28
MACARONI AND CHEESE	25
MAKE AHEAD CHEESY MASHED POTATOES	27
MARINATED CARROTS	23
MOTHER'S SQUASH CASSEROLE	29
PICKLED CARROT DISH	24
PINEAPPLE BREAD CASSEROLE	26
POTATO CASSEROLE	28
RICE CASSEROLE	29
SOUTHERN MASHED POTATOES	28
SQUASH CASSEROLE	29
SWEET POTATO AND APPLE CASSEROLE	30
SWEET POTATO CASSEROLE	30
TOMATO PIE	31
VIDALIA ONION PIE	26
YORKSHIRE PUDDING	31

92567A-08 1

MAIN DISHES

BROCCOLI-CHICKEN CASSEROLE	34
CAROL'S CASSEROLE	34
CHEESE GRITS AND SHRIMP CASSEROLE	47
CHICKEN AND DUMPLINGS	37
CHICKEN AND RICE CASSEROLE	36
CHICKEN & STUFFING BAKE	37
CHICKEN CASSEROLE	34
CHICKEN PARMESAN	35
CHICKEN POT PIE	36
CHICKEN TETRAZINNI	39
CHICKEN WRAPPED IN BACON	35
COMFORTING CHICKEN CASSEROLE	38
CONNIE'S CHICKEN CASSEROLE	35
CRAZY CHICKEN OR TURKEY PIE	38
EASY SHRIMP CREOLE	48
FAMILY CHILI	40
FAVORITE POT ROAST	43
FLORIDA SEAFOOD CASSEROLE	44
GREEK SPINACH AND CHEESE PIE	46
HAM AND EGG QUICHE	40
HAMBURGER CASSEROLE	40
HAMBURGER STROGANOFF	41
ITALIAN BEEF 'N CHEESE DINNER	33
LASAGNA	41
MAKE AHEAD BREAKFAST CASSEROLE	33
MEAT LOAF	42
MEXICAN DINNER	42
ONE DISH CHICKEN & RICE BAKE	37
PEPPER STEAK WITH RICE	43
POMEROY'S FAVORITE LASAGNA	41
POPPY SEED CHICKEN	39
PORK CHOPS AND PEAS	46
SALMON CROQUETTE	43
SAUSAGE RICE CASSEROLE	44
SHEPHERD'S PIE	44
SHRIMP CASSEROLE	47
SOUTHERN FRIED CHICKEN	39
SPAGHETTI MEAT SAUCE	45
SPAGHETTI PIE	45
SPARERIBS AND SAUERKRAUT	46
STEWED CHICKEN	36
STUFFED SHELLS	48
TAMALE PIE	48
VEAL SCALOPPINI	49

BREADS & ROLLS

APPLE MUFFINS	51
APRICOT BANANA BREAD	51
BANANA NUT BREAD	52
BANANA WALNUT MUFFINS	52
BLUEBERRY MUFFINS	52
BRAN MUFFINS	53
CRANBERRY NUT BREAD	53
CRUNCHY CHEESE BISCUITS	53
DATE NUT BREAD	54
HOT MEXICAN BREAD	55
OATMEAL MUFFINS	55
PINEAPPLE NUT BREAD	56
PULL-APART VEGETABLE BREAD	57
PUMPKIN BREAD	56
QUICK LEMONADE BREAD	54
QUICK MAYONNAISE ROLLS	54
STICKY BUNS	56
STRAWBERRY NUT BREAD	57
ZUCCHINI NUT BREAD	57

DESSERTS

A FAVORITE 4-LAYER DESSERT	73
APPLE CAKE	59
APPLESAUCE CAKE	60
BANANA CAKE	60
BANANA CREAM PIE	74
BANANA FROSTING	61
BANANA ICE CREAM	81
BEST CARROT CAKE	62
BLACKBERRY PIE	75
BUTTER PECAN ICE CREAM	81
BUTTERMILK POUND CAKE	68
CHEESECAKE	76
CHERRY CHEESECAKE	76
CHOCOLATE COCOA COLA CAKE	62
CHOCOLATE DISAPPEARING CAKE	63
CHOCOLATE MORSEL PIE	77
CHOCOLATE SHEET CAKE	63
COCONUT CAKE	63
COCONUT CREAM PIE	75
COCONUT CUSTARD PIE	75
CONFECTIONER SUGAR POUND CAKE	68
CREAM CARAMEL CAKE	64
EASY DOES IT PEANUT BUTTER PIE	79
FRESH APPLE CAKE	59
GEORGIA POUND CAKE	68
GERMAN CHOCOLATE CAKE	64
GINGERBREAD	65
GOOD MORNING CAKE	65

GREAT CARROT CAKE	61
HOT FUDGE PUDDING CAKE	66
ICE CREAM PIE AND SAUCE	77
ICEBOX PIE	77
JAPANESE FRUITCAKE	66
KEY LIME PIE	78
LEMON ICEBOX PIE	78
MANDARIN ORANGE CAKE	67
MOTHER'S BANANA PUDDING	74
OATMEAL PIE	78
OLD-STYLE POUND CAKE	69
ORANGE CARROT CAKE	69
PEACH COBBLER	79
PEAR NECTAR-CHERRY DELIGHT CAKE	70
PECAN PIE	79
PUMPKIN CAKE WITH CREAM CHEESE FROSTING	70
RUM CAKE AND SAUCE	71
7-UP CAKE	73
SOUR CREAM POUND CAKE	71
SOUTHERN LANE CAKE	67
STRAWBERRY CARROT CAKE	72
STRAWBERRY SHORTCUT CAKE	72
SWEET POTATO PIE	80
VANILLA ICE CREAM	81
WALNUT PUMPKIN PIE	80

COOKIES & CANDY

BLONDE BROWNIES	83
BROWNIES	83
BUTTER ALMOND CRESCENT COOKIES	84
BUTTERSCOTCH BABBLES	85
CHESS CAKE SQUARES	86
CHOCOLATE CHIP MERINGUE COOKIES	91
CHOCOLATE COW PIES	85
CHOCOLATE CRINKLE COOKIES	85
CHOCOLATE-PEANUT BUTTER FUDGE	87
COCOA FUDGE	88
CRACKER SNACK	87
CREAMY PRALINES	96
DATE PECAN ROLL	88
DELICIOUS CINNAMON ROLL-UPS	86
DIVINITY	89
EASY CRACKER TREAT	86
ENGLISH TOFFEE	89
FRUIT CAKE COOKIES	90
FUDGE	87
FUDGE BROWNIES	84
JELLY TOTS COOKIES	90
LEMON SQUARES	90

LEMONY CHEESECAKE SQUARES	91
MOTHER'S DATE NUT ROLL	88
NO-BAKE CHOCOLATE OATMEAL COOKIES	86
OATMEAL DROP COOKIES	92
OATMEAL FUDGE BARS	92
PEANUT BUTTER COOKIES	92
PEANUT BUTTER MIDDLES	93
PEANUT BUTTER TEA CAKES	93
PECAN BALLS	94
PECAN PIE BARS	94
PECAN PIE COOKIES	94
PEOPLE CHOW	95
PEPPERMINT COOKIES	95
POTATO CHIP COOKIES	96
PRALINES	96
ROCKY ROAD FUDGE BARS	97
ROCKY ROAD SQUARES	98
RUM BALLS	98
SNOW FLAKES	98
SPICY PUMPKIN BARS	97

THIS & THAT

CAROL'S SPICED PECANS	101
GARLIC RUB	101
HOMEMADE MAYONNAISE	101
HONEY-MUSTARD DRESSING	104
MANDARIN ORANGE VINAIGRETTE	104
PEPPER JELLY	102
RASPBERRY VINAIGRETTE	104
SEVEN-MINUTE ICING	102
SHRIMP BUTTER	102
STIR-DROP DOUGHNUTS	103
WAFFLES	103
WHITE BARBECUE SAUCE	103

How to Order

Get additional copies of this cookbook by returning an order form and your check or money order to:

Patsy Pomeroy
2411 63rd St. W.
Bradenton, FL 34209
r_pomeroy@msn.com

Please send me _____ copies of **Three Sisters from the South** at **$14.95** per copy and **$3.00** for shipping and handling per book. Enclosed is my check or money order for $_____.

Mail Books To:

Name _____

Address _____

City _____ State _____ Zip _____

Please send me _____ copies of **Three Sisters from the South** at **$14.95** per copy and **$3.00** for shipping and handling per book. Enclosed is my check or money order for $_____.

Mail Books To:

Name _____

Address _____

City _____ State _____ Zip _____

92567-dl

PANTRY BASICS

A WELL-STOCKED PANTRY provides all the makings for a good meal. With the right ingredients, you can quickly create a variety of satisfying, delicious meals for family or guests. Keeping these items in stock also means avoiding extra trips to the grocery store, saving you time and money. Although everyone's pantry is different, there are basic items you should always have. Add other items according to your family's needs. For example, while some families consider chips, cereals and snacks as must-haves, others can't be without feta cheese and imported olives. Use these basic pantry suggestions as a handy reference list when creating your grocery list. Don't forget refrigerated items like milk, eggs, cheese and butter.

STAPLES

Baker's chocolate
Baking powder
Baking soda
Barbeque sauce
Bread crumbs (plain or seasoned)
Chocolate chips
Cocoa powder
Cornmeal
Cornstarch
Crackers
Flour
Honey
Ketchup
Lemon juice
Mayonnaise or salad dressing
Non-stick cooking spray
Nuts (almonds, pecans, walnuts)
Oatmeal
Oil (olive, vegetable)
Pancake baking mix
Pancake syrup
Peanut butter
Shortening
Sugar (granulated, brown, powdered)
Vinegar

PACKAGED/CANNED FOODS

Beans (canned, dry)
Broth (beef, chicken)
Cake mixes with frosting
Canned diced tomatoes
Canned fruit
Canned mushrooms
Canned soup
Canned tomato paste & sauce
Canned tuna & chicken
Cereal
Dried soup mix
Gelatin (flavored or plain)
Gravies
Jarred Salsa
Milk (evaporated, sweetened condensed)
Non-fat dry milk
Pastas
Rice (brown, white)
Spaghetti sauce

SPICES/SEASONINGS

Basil
Bay leaves
Black pepper
Bouillon cubes (beef, chicken)
Chives
Chili powder
Cinnamon
Mustard (dried, prepared)
Garlic powder or salt
Ginger
Nutmeg
Onion powder or salt
Oregano
Paprika
Parsley
Rosemary
Sage
Salt
Soy sauce
Tarragon
Thyme
Vanilla
Worcestershire sauce
Yeast

Copyright © 2006
Morris Press Cookbooks
All Rights Reserved.

HERBS & SPICES

DRIED VS. FRESH. While dried herbs are convenient, they don't generally have the same purity of flavor as fresh herbs. Ensure dried herbs are still fresh by checking if they are green and not faded. Crush a few leaves to see if the aroma is still strong. Always store them in an air-tight container away from light and heat.

BASIL — Sweet, warm flavor with an aromatic odor. Use whole or ground. Good with lamb, fish, roast, stews, beef, vegetables, dressing and omelets.

BAY LEAVES — Pungent flavor. Use whole leaf but remove before serving. Good in vegetable dishes, seafood, stews and pickles.

CARAWAY — Spicy taste and aromatic smell. Use in cakes, breads, soups, cheese and sauerkraut.

CELERY SEED — Strong taste which resembles the vegetable. Can be used sparingly in pickles and chutney, meat and fish dishes, salads, bread, marinades, dressings and dips.

CHIVES — Sweet, mild flavor like that of onion. Excellent in salads, fish, soups and potatoes.

CILANTRO — Use fresh. Excellent in salads, fish, chicken, rice, beans and Mexican dishes.

CINNAMON — Sweet, pungent flavor. Widely used in many sweet baked goods, chocolate dishes, cheesecakes, pickles, chutneys and hot drinks.

CORIANDER — Mild, sweet, orangy flavor and available whole or ground. Common in curry powders and pickling spice and also used in chutney, meat dishes, casseroles, Greek-style dishes, apple pies and baked goods.

CURRY POWDER — Spices are combined to proper proportions to give a distinct flavor to meat, poultry, fish and vegetables.

DILL — Both seeds and leaves are flavorful. Leaves may be used as a garnish or cooked with fish, soup, dressings, potatoes and beans. Leaves or the whole plant may be used to flavor pickles.

FENNEL — Sweet, hot flavor. Both seeds and leaves are used. Use in small quantities in pies and baked goods. Leaves can be boiled with fish.

HERBS & SPICES

GINGER — A pungent root, this aromatic spice is sold fresh, dried or ground. Use in pickles, preserves, cakes, cookies, soups and meat dishes.

MARJORAM — May be used both dried or green. Use to flavor fish, poultry, omelets, lamb, stew, stuffing and tomato juice.

MINT — Aromatic with a cool flavor. Excellent in beverages, fish, lamb, cheese, soup, peas, carrots and fruit desserts.

NUTMEG — Whole or ground. Used in chicken and cream soups, cheese dishes, fish cakes, and with chicken and veal. Excellent in custards, milk puddings, pies and cakes.

OREGANO — Strong, aromatic odor. Use whole or ground in tomato juice, fish, eggs, pizza, omelets, chili, stew, gravy, poultry and vegetables.

PAPRIKA — A bright red pepper, this spice is used in meat, vegetables and soups or as a garnish for potatoes, salads or eggs.

PARSLEY — Best when used fresh, but can be used dried as a garnish or as a seasoning. Try in fish, omelets, soup, meat, stuffing and mixed greens.

ROSEMARY — Very aromatic. Can be used fresh or dried. Season fish, stuffing, beef, lamb, poultry, onions, eggs, bread and potatoes. Great in dressings.

SAFFRON — Aromatic, slightly bitter taste. Only a pinch needed to flavor and color dishes such as bouillabaisse, chicken soup, rice, paella, fish sauces, buns and cakes. Very expensive, so where a touch of color is needed, use turmeric instead, but the flavor will not be the same.

SAGE — Use fresh or dried. The flowers are sometimes used in salads. May be used in tomato juice, fish, omelets, beef, poultry, stuffing, cheese spreads and breads.

TARRAGON — Leaves have a pungent, hot taste. Use to flavor sauces, salads, fish, poultry, tomatoes, eggs, green beans, carrots and dressings.

THYME — Sprinkle leaves on fish or poultry before broiling or baking. Throw a few sprigs directly on coals shortly before meat is finished grilling.

TURMERIC — Aromatic, slightly bitter flavor. Should be used sparingly in curry powder and relishes and to color cakes and rice dishes.

Use 3 times more fresh herbs if substituting fresh for dried.

BAKING BREADS

HINTS FOR BAKING BREADS

- Kneading dough for 30 seconds after mixing improves the texture of baking powder biscuits.

- Instead of shortening, use cooking or salad oil in waffles and hot cakes.

- When bread is baking, a small dish of water in the oven will help keep the crust from hardening.

- Dip a spoon in hot water to measure shortening, butter, etc., and the fat will slip out more easily.

- Small amounts of leftover corn may be added to pancake batter for variety.

- To make bread crumbs, use the fine cutter of a food grinder and tie a large paper bag over the spout in order to prevent flying crumbs.

- When you are doing any sort of baking, you get better results if you remember to preheat your cookie sheet, muffin tins or cake pans.

3 RULES FOR USE OF LEAVENING AGENTS

1. In simple flour mixtures, use 2 teaspoons baking powder to leaven 1 cup flour. Reduce this amount 1/2 teaspoon for each egg used.

2. To 1 teaspoon soda, use 2 1/4 teaspoons cream of tartar, 2 cups freshly soured milk or 1 cup molasses.

3. To substitute soda and an acid for baking powder, divide the amount of baking powder by 4. Take that as your measure and add acid according to rule 2.

PROPORTIONS OF BAKING POWDER TO FLOUR

biscuits	to 1 cup flour use 1 1/4 tsp. baking powder
cake with oil	to 1 cup flour use 1 tsp. baking powder
muffins	to 1 cup flour use 1 1/2 tsp. baking powder
popovers	to 1 cup flour use 1 1/4 tsp. baking powder
waffles	to 1 cup flour use 1 1/4 tsp. baking powder

PROPORTIONS OF LIQUID TO FLOUR

pour batter	to 1 cup liquid use 1 cup flour
drop batter	to 1 cup liquid use 2 to 2 1/2 cups flour
soft dough	to 1 cup liquid use 3 to 3 1/2 cups flour
stiff dough	to 1 cup liquid use 4 cups flour

TIME & TEMPERATURE CHART

Breads	Minutes	Temperature
biscuits	12 - 15	400° - 450°
cornbread	25 - 30	400° - 425°
gingerbread	40 - 50	350° - 370°
loaf	50 - 60	350° - 400°
nut bread	50 - 75	350°
popovers	30 - 40	425° - 450°
rolls	20 - 30	400° - 450°

BAKING DESSERTS

PERFECT COOKIES

Cookie dough that must be rolled is much easier to handle after it has been refrigerated for 10 to 30 minutes. This keeps the dough from sticking, even though it may be soft. If not done, the soft dough may require more flour and too much flour makes cookies hard and brittle. Place on a floured board only as much dough as can be easily managed. Flour the rolling pin slightly and roll lightly to desired thickness. Cut shapes close together and add trimmings to dough that needs to be rolled. Place pans or sheets in upper third of oven. Watch cookies carefully while baking in order to avoid burned edges. When sprinkling sugar on cookies, try putting it into a salt shaker in order to save time.

PERFECT PIES

- Pie crust will be better and easier to make if all the ingredients are cool.

- The lower crust should be placed in the pan so that it covers the surface smoothly. Air pockets beneath the surface will push the crust out of shape while baking.

- Folding the top crust over the lower crust before crimping will keep juices in the pie.

- When making custard pie, bake at a high temperature for about 10 minutes to prevent a soggy crust. Then finish baking at a low temperature.

- When making cream pie, sprinkle crust with powdered sugar in order to prevent it from becoming soggy.

PERFECT CAKES

- Fill cake pans two-thirds full and spread batter into corners and sides, leaving a slight hollow in the center.

- Cake is done when it shrinks from the sides of the pan or if it springs back when touched lightly with the finger.

- After removing a cake from the oven, place it on a rack for about 5 minutes. Then, the sides should be loosened and the cake turned out on a rack in order to finish cooling.

- Do not frost cakes until thoroughly cool.

- Icing will remain where you put it if you sprinkle cake with powdered sugar first.

TIME & TEMPERATURE CHART

Dessert	Time	Temperature
butter cake, layer	20-40 min.	380° - 400°
butter cake, loaf	40-60 min.	360° - 400°
cake, angel	50-60 min.	300° - 360°
cake, fruit	3-4 hrs.	275° - 325°
cake, sponge	40-60 min.	300° - 350°
cookies, molasses	18-20 min.	350° - 375°
cookies, thin	10-12 min.	380° - 390°
cream puffs	45-60 min.	300° - 350°
meringue	40-60 min.	250° - 300°
pie crust	20-40 min.	400° - 500°

VEGETABLES & FRUITS

COOKING TIME TABLE

Vegetable	Cooking Method	Time
artichokes	boiled	40 min.
	steamed	45-60 min.
asparagus tips	boiled	10-15 min.
beans, lima	boiled	20-40 min.
	steamed	60 min.
beans, string	boiled	15-35 min.
	steamed	60 min.
beets, old	boiled or steamed	1-2 hours.
beets, young with skin	boiled	30 min.
	steamed	60 min.
	baked	70-90 min.
broccoli, flowerets	boiled	5-10 min.
broccoli, stems	boiled	20-30 min.
brussels sprouts	boiled	20-30 min.
cabbage, chopped	boiled	10-20 min.
	steamed	25 min.
carrots, cut across	boiled	8-10 min.
	steamed	40 min.
cauliflower, flowerets	boiled	8-10 min.
cauliflower, stem down	boiled	20-30 min.
corn, green, tender	boiled	5-10 min.
	steamed	15 min.
	baked	20 min.
corn on the cob	boiled	8-10 min.
	steamed	15 min.
eggplant, whole	boiled	30 min.
	steamed	40 min.
	baked	45 min.
parsnips	boiled	25-40 min.
	steamed	60 min.
	baked	60-75 min.
peas, green	boiled or steamed	5-15 min.
potatoes	boiled	20-40 min.
	steamed	60 min.
	baked	45-60 min.
pumpkin or squash	boiled	20-40 min.
	steamed	45 min.
	baked	60 min.
tomatoes	boiled	5-15 min.
turnips	boiled	25-40 min.

DRYING TIME TABLE

Fruit	Sugar or Honey	Cooking Time
apricots	1/4 c. for each cup of fruit	about 40 min.
figs	1 T. for each cup of fruit	about 30 min.
peaches	1/4 c. for each cup of fruit	about 45 min.
prunes	2 T. for each cup of fruit	about 45 min.

VEGETABLES & FRUITS

BUYING FRESH VEGETABLES

Artichokes: Look for compact, tightly closed heads with green, clean-looking leaves. Avoid those with leaves that are brown or separated.

Asparagus: Stalks should be tender and firm; tips should be close and compact. Choose the stalks with very little white; they are more tender. Use asparagus soon because it toughens quickly.

Beans, Snap: Those with small seeds inside the pods are best. Avoid beans with dry-looking pods.

Broccoli, Brussels Sprouts and Cauliflower: Flower clusters on broccoli and cauliflower should be tight and close together. Brussels sprouts should be firm and compact. Smudgy, dirty spots may indicate pests or disease.

Cabbage and Head Lettuce: Choose heads that are heavy for their size. Avoid cabbage with worm holes and lettuce with discoloration or soft rot.

Cucumbers: Choose long, slender cucumbers for best quality. May be dark or medium green, but yellow ones are undesirable.

Mushrooms: Caps should be closed around the stems. Avoid black or brown gills.

Peas and Lima Beans: Select pods that are well-filled but not bulging. Avoid dried, spotted, yellow or limp pods.

BUYING FRESH FRUITS

Bananas: Skin should be free of bruises and black or brown spots. Purchase them slightly green and allow them to ripen at room temperature.

Berries: Select plump, solid berries with good color. Avoid stained containers which indicate wet or leaky berries. Berries with clinging caps, such as blackberries and raspberries, may be unripe. Strawberries without caps may be overripe.

Melons: In cantaloupes, thick, close netting on the rind indicates best quality. Cantaloupes are ripe when the stem scar is smooth and the space between the netting is yellow or yellow-green. They are best when fully ripe with fruity odor.

Honeydews are ripe when rind has creamy to yellowish color and velvety texture. Immature honeydews are whitish-green.

Ripe watermelons have some yellow color on one side. If melons are white or pale green on one side, they are not ripe.

Oranges, Grapefruit and Lemons: Choose those heavy for their size. Smoother, thinner skins usually indicate more juice. Most skin markings do not affect quality. Oranges with a slight greenish tinge may be just as ripe as fully colored ones. Light or greenish-yellow lemons are more tart than deep yellow ones. Avoid citrus fruits showing withered, sunken or soft areas.

NAPKIN FOLDING

FOR BEST RESULTS, use well-starched linen napkins if possible. For more complicated folds, 24-inch napkins work best. Practice the folds with newspapers. Children will have fun decorating the table once they learn these attractive folds!

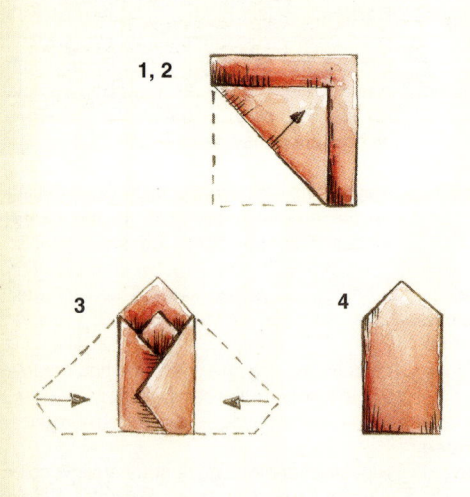

SHIELD

Easy fold. Elegant with monogram in corner.

Instructions:
1. Fold into quarter size. If monogrammed, ornate corner should face down.
2. Turn up folded corner three-quarters.
3. Overlap right side and left side points.
4. Turn over; adjust sides so they are even, single point in center.
5. Place point up or down on plate, or left of plate.

ROSETTE

Elegant on plate.

Instructions:
1. Fold left and right edges to center, leaving 1/2" opening along center.
2. Pleat firmly from top edge to bottom edge. Sharpen edges with hot iron.
3. Pinch center together. If necessary, use small piece of pipe cleaner to secure and top with single flower.
4. Spread out rosette.

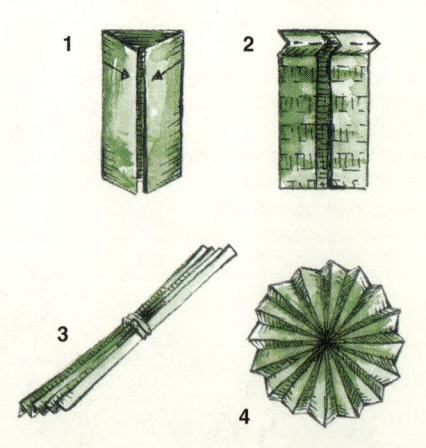

NAPKIN FOLDING

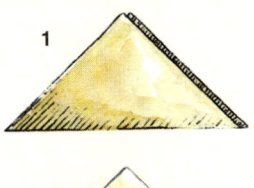

CANDLE

Easy to do; can be decorated.

Instructions:
1. Fold into triangle, point at top.
2. Turn lower edge up 1".
3. Turn over, folded edge down.
4. Roll tightly from left to right.
5. Tuck in corner. Stand upright.

FAN

Pretty in napkin ring or on plate.

Instructions:
1. Fold top and bottom edges to center.
2. Fold top and bottom edges to center a second time.
3. Pleat firmly from the left edge. Sharpen edges with hot iron.
4. Spread out fan. Balance flat folds of each side on table. Well-starched napkins will hold shape.

LILY

Effective and pretty on table.

Instructions:
1. Fold napkin into quarters.
2. Fold into triangle, closed corner to open points.
3. Turn two points over to other side. (Two points are on either side of closed point.)
4. Pleat.
5. Place closed end in glass. Pull down two points on each side and shape.

MEASUREMENTS & SUBSTITUTIONS

MEASUREMENTS

a pinch	1/8 teaspoon or less
3 teaspoons	1 tablespoon
4 tablespoons	1/4 cup
8 tablespoons	1/2 cup
12 tablespoons	3/4 cup
16 tablespoons	1 cup
2 cups	1 pint
4 cups	1 quart
4 quarts	1 gallon
8 quarts	1 peck
4 pecks	1 bushel
16 ounces	1 pound
32 ounces	1 quart
1 ounce liquid	2 tablespoons
8 ounces liquid	1 cup

Use standard measuring spoons and cups. All measurements are level.

C° TO F° CONVERSION

120° C	250° F
140° C	275° F
150° C	300° F
160° C	325° F
180° C	350° F
190° C	375° F
200° C	400° F
220° C	425° F
230° C	450° F

Temperature conversions are estimates.

SUBSTITUTIONS

Ingredient	Quantity	Substitute
baking powder	1 teaspoon	1/4 tsp. baking soda plus 1/2 tsp. cream of tartar
chocolate	1 square (1 oz.)	3 or 4 T. cocoa plus 1 T. butter
cornstarch	1 tablespoon	2 T. flour or 2 tsp. quick-cooking tapioca
cracker crumbs	3/4 cup	1 c. bread crumbs
dates	1 lb.	1 1/2 c. dates, pitted and cut
dry mustard	1 teaspoon	1 T. prepared mustard
flour, self-rising	1 cup	1 c. all-purpose flour, 1/2 tsp. salt, and 1 tsp. baking powder
herbs, fresh	1 tablespoon	1 tsp. dried herbs
ketchup or chili sauce	1 cup	1 c. tomato sauce plus 1/2 c. sugar and 2 T. vinegar (for use in cooking)
milk, sour	1 cup	1 T. lemon juice or vinegar plus sweet milk to make 1 c. (let stand 5 minutes)
whole	1 cup	1/2 c. evaporated milk plus 1/2 c. water
min. marshmallows	10	1 lg. marshmallow
onion, fresh	1 small	1 T. instant minced onion, rehydrated
sugar, brown	1/2 cup	2 T. molasses in 1/2 c. granulated sugar
powdered	1 cup	1 c. granulated sugar plus 1 tsp. cornstarch
tomato juice	1 cup	1/2 c. tomato sauce plus 1/2 c. water

When substituting cocoa for chocolate in cakes, the amount of flour must be reduced. Brown and white sugars usually can be interchanged.

EQUIVALENCY CHART

Food	Quantity	Yield
apple	1 medium	1 cup
banana, mashed	1 medium	1/3 cup
bread	1 1/2 slices	1 cup soft crumbs
bread	1 slice	1/4 cup fine, dry crumbs
butter	1 stick or 1/4 pound	1/2 cup
cheese, American, cubed	1 pound	2 2/3 cups
American, grated	1 pound	5 cups
cream cheese	3-ounce package	6 2/3 tablespoons
chocolate, bitter	1 square	1 ounce
cocoa	1 pound	4 cups
coconut	1 1/2 pound package	2 2/3 cups
coffee, ground	1 pound	5 cups
cornmeal	1 pound	3 cups
cornstarch	1 pound	3 cups
crackers, graham	14 squares	1 cup fine crumbs
saltine	28 crackers	1 cup fine crumbs
egg	4-5 whole	1 cup
whites	8-10	1 cup
yolks	10-12	1 cup
evaporated milk	1 cup	3 cups whipped
flour, cake, sifted	1 pound	4 1/2 cups
rye	1 pound	5 cups
white, sifted	1 pound	4 cups
white, unsifted	1 pound	3 3/4 cups
gelatin, flavored	3 1/4 ounces	1/2 cup
unflavored	1/4 ounce	1 tablespoon
lemon	1 medium	3 tablespoon juice
marshmallows	16	1/4 pound
noodles, cooked	8-ounce package	7 cups
uncooked	4 ounces (1 1/2 cups)	2-3 cups cooked
macaroni, cooked	8-ounce package	6 cups
macaroni, uncooked	4 ounces (1 1/4 cups)	2 1/4 cups cooked
spaghetti, uncooked	7 ounces	4 cups cooked
nuts, chopped	1/4 pound	1 cup
almonds	1 pound	3 1/2 cups
walnuts, broken	1 pound	3 cups
walnuts, unshelled	1 pound	1 1/2 to 1 3/4 cups
onion	1 medium	1/2 cup
orange	3-4 medium	1 cup juice
raisins	1 pound	3 1/2 cups
rice, brown	1 cup	4 cups cooked
converted	1 cup	3 1/2 cups cooked
regular	1 cup	3 cups cooked
wild	1 cup	4 cups cooked
sugar, brown	1 pound	2 1/2 cups
powdered	1 pound	3 1/2 cups
white	1 pound	2 cups
vanilla wafers	22	1 cup fine crumbs
zwieback, crumbled	4	1 cups

FOOD QUANTITIES

FOR LARGE SERVINGS

	25 Servings	50 Servings	100 Servings
Beverages:			
coffee	1/2 pound and 1 1/2 gallons water	1 pound and 3 gallons water	2 pounds and 6 gallons water
lemonade	10-15 lemons and 1 1/2 gallons water	20-30 lemons and 3 gallons water	40-60 lemons and 6 gallons water
tea	1/12 pound and 1 1/2 gallons water	1/6 pound and 3 gallons water	1/3 pound and 6 gallons water
Desserts:			
layered cake	1 12" cake	3 10" cakes	6 10" cakes
sheet cake	1 10" x 12" cake	1 12" x 20" cake	2 12" x 20" cakes
watermelon	37 1/2 pounds	75 pounds	150 pounds
whipping cream	3/4 pint	1 1/2 to 2 pints	3-4 pints
Ice cream:			
brick	3 1/4 quarts	6 1/2 quarts	13 quarts
bulk	2 1/4 quarts	4 1/2 quarts or 1 1/4 gallons	9 quarts or 2 1/2 gallons
Meat, poultry or fish:			
fish	13 pounds	25 pounds	50 pounds
fish, fillets or steak	7 1/2 pounds	15 pounds	30 pounds
hamburger	9 pounds	18 pounds	35 pounds
turkey or chicken	13 pounds	25 to 35 pounds	50 to 75 pounds
wieners (beef)	6 1/2 pounds	13 pounds	25 pounds
Salads, casseroles:			
baked beans	3/4 gallon	1 1/4 gallons	2 1/2 gallons
jello salad	3/4 gallon	1 1/4 gallons	2 1/2 gallons
potato salad	4 1/4 quarts	2 1/4 gallons	4 1/2 gallons
scalloped potatoes	4 1/2 quarts or 1 12" x 20" pan	9 quarts or 2 1/4 gallons	18 quarts 4 1/2 gallons
spaghetti	1 1/4 gallons	2 1/2 gallons	5 gallons
Sandwiches:			
bread	50 slices or 3 1-pound loaves	100 slices or 6 1-pound loaves	200 slices or 12 1-pound loaves
butter	1/2 pound	1 pound	2 pounds
lettuce	1 1/2 heads	3 heads	6 heads
mayonnaise	1 cup	2 cups	4 cups
mixed filling			
meat, eggs, fish	1 1/2 quarts	3 quarts	6 quarts
jam, jelly	1 quart	2 quarts	4 quarts

QUICK FIXES

PRACTICALLY EVERYONE has experienced that dreadful moment in the kitchen when a recipe failed and dinner guests have arrived. Perhaps a failed timer, distraction or a missing or mismeasured ingredient is to blame. These handy tips can save the day!

Acidic foods – Sometimes a tomato-based sauce will become too acidic. Add baking soda, one teaspoon at a time, to the sauce. Use sugar as a sweeter alternative.

Burnt food on pots and pans – Allow the pan to cool on its own. Remove as much of the food as possible. Fill with hot water and add a capful of liquid fabric softener to the pot; let it stand for a few hours. You'll have an easier time removing the burnt food.

Chocolate seizes – Chocolate can seize (turn coarse and grainy) when it comes into contact with water. Place seized chocolate in a metal bowl over a large saucepan with an inch of simmering water in it. Over medium heat, slowly whisk in warm heavy cream. Use 1/4 cup cream to 4 ounces of chocolate. The chocolate will melt and become smooth.

Forgot to thaw whipped topping – Thaw in microwave for 1 minute on the defrost setting. Stir to blend well. Do not over thaw!

Hands smell like garlic or onion – Rinse hands under cold water while rubbing them with a large stainless steel spoon.

Hard brown sugar – Place in a paper bag and microwave for a few seconds, or place hard chunks in a food processor.

Jello too hard – Heat on a low microwave power setting for a very short time.

Lumpy gravy or sauce – Use a blender, food processor or simply strain.

No tomato juice – Mix 1/2 cup ketchup with 1/2 cup water.

Out of honey – Substitute 1 1/4 cups sugar dissolved in 1 cup water.

Overcooked sweet potatoes or carrots – Softened sweet potatoes and carrots make a wonderful soufflé with the addition of eggs and sugar. Consult your favorite cookbook for a good soufflé recipe. Overcooked sweet potatoes can also be used as pie filling.

Sandwich bread is stale – Toast or microwave bread briefly. Otherwise, turn it into breadcrumbs. Bread exposed to light and heat will hasten its demise, so consider using a bread box.

Soup, sauce, gravy too thin – Add 1 tablespoon of flour to hot soup, sauce or gravy. Whisk well (to avoid lumps) while the mixture is boiling. Repeat if necessary.

Sticky rice – Rinse rice with warm water.

Stew or soup is greasy – Refrigerate and remove grease once it congeals. Another trick is to lay cold lettuce leaves over the hot stew for about 10 seconds and then remove. Repeat as necessary.

Too salty – Add a little sugar and vinegar. For soups or sauces, add a raw peeled potato.

Too sweet – Add a little vinegar or lemon juice.

Undercooked cakes and cookies – Serve over vanilla ice cream. You can also layer pieces of cake or cookies with whipped cream and fresh fruit to form a dessert parfait. Crumbled cookies also make an excellent ice cream or cream pie topping.

COUNTING CALORIES

BEVERAGES

apple juice, 6 oz.	90
coffee (black)	0
cola, 12 oz.	115
cranberry juice, 6 oz.	115
ginger ale, 12 oz.	115
grape juice, (prepared from frozen concentrate), 6 oz.	142
lemonade, (prepared from frozen concentrate), 6 oz.	85
milk, protein fortified, 1 c.	105
skim, 1 c.	90
whole, 1 c.	160
orange juice, 6 oz.	85
pineapple juice, unsweetened, 6 oz.	95
root beer, 12 oz.	150
tonic (quinine water) 12 oz.	132

BREADS

cornbread, 1 sm. square	130
dumplings, 1 med.	70
French toast, 1 slice	135
melba toast, 1 slice	25
muffins, blueberry, 1 muffin	110
bran, 1 muffin	106
corn, 1 muffin	125
English, 1 muffin	280
pancakes, 1 (4-in.)	60
pumpernickel, 1 slice	75
rye, 1 slice	60
waffle, 1	216
white, 1 slice	60-70
whole wheat, 1 slice	55-65

CEREALS

cornflakes, 1 c.	105
cream of wheat, 1 c.	120
oatmeal, 1 c.	148
rice flakes, 1 c.	105
shredded wheat, 1 biscuit	100
sugar krisps, ¾ c.	110

CRACKERS

graham, 1 cracker	15-30
rye crisp, 1 cracker	35
saltine, 1 cracker	17-20
wheat thins, 1 cracker	9

DAIRY PRODUCTS

butter or margarine, 1 T.	100
cheese, American, 1 oz.	100
camembert, 1 oz.	85
cheddar, 1 oz.	115
cottage cheese, 1 oz.	30
mozzarella, 1 oz.	90
parmesan, 1 oz.	130
ricotta, 1 oz.	50
roquefort, 1 oz.	105
Swiss, 1 oz.	105
cream, light, 1 T.	30
heavy, 1 T.	55
sour, 1 T.	45
hot chocolate, with milk, 1 c.	277
milk chocolate, 1 oz.	145-155
yogurt	
made w/ whole milk, 1 c.	150-165
made w/ skimmed milk, 1 c.	125

EGGS

fried, 1 lg.	100
poached or boiled, 1 lg.	75-80
scrambled or in omelet, 1 lg.	110-130

FISH AND SEAFOOD

bass, 4 oz.	105
salmon, broiled or baked, 3 oz.	155
sardines, canned in oil, 3 oz.	170
trout, fried, 3 ½ oz.	220
tuna, in oil, 3 oz.	170
in water, 3 oz.	110

COUNTING CALORIES

FRUITS

apple, 1 med. 80-100
applesauce, sweetened, 1/2 c. 90-115
    unsweetened, 1/2 c. 50
banana, 1 med. 85
blueberries, 1/2 c. 45
cantaloupe, 1/2 c. 24
cherries (pitted), raw, 1/2 c. 40
grapefruit, 1/2 med. 55
grapes, 1/2 c. 35-55
honeydew, 1/2 c. 55
mango, 1 med. 90
orange, 1 med. 65-75
peach, 1 med. 35
pear, 1 med. 60-100
pineapple, fresh, 1/2 c. 40
    canned in syrup, 1/2 c. 95
plum, 1 med. 30
strawberries, fresh, 1/2 c. 30
    frozen and sweetened, 1/2 c. ..120-140
tangerine, 1 lg. 39
watermelon, 1/2 c. 42

MEAT AND POULTRY

beef, ground (lean), 3 oz. 185
    roast, 3 oz. 185
chicken, broiled, 3 oz. 115
lamb chop (lean), 3 oz. 175-200
steak, sirloin, 3 oz. 175
    tenderloin, 3 oz. 174
    top round, 3 oz. 162
turkey, dark meat, 3 oz. 175
    white meat, 3 oz. 150
veal, cutlet, 3 oz. 156
    roast, 3 oz. 76

NUTS

almonds, 2 T. 105
cashews, 2 T. 100
peanuts, 2 T. 105
peanut butter, 1 T. 95
pecans, 2 T. 95
pistachios, 2 T. 92
walnuts, 2 T. 80

PASTA

macaroni or spaghetti,
    cooked, 3/4 c. 115

SALAD DRESSINGS

blue cheese, 1 T. 70
French, 1 T. 65
Italian, 1 T. 80
mayonnaise, 1 T. 100
olive oil, 1 T. 124
Russian, 1 T. 70
salad oil, 1 T. 120

SOUPS

bean, 1 c. 130-180
beef noodle, 1 c. 70
bouillon and consomme, 1 c. 30
chicken noodle, 1 c. 65
chicken with rice, 1 c. 50
minestrone, 1 c. 80-150
split pea, 1 c. 145-170
tomato with milk, 1 c. 170
vegetable, 1 c. 80-100

VEGETABLES

asparagus, 1 c. 35
broccoli, cooked, 1/2 c. 25
cabbage, cooked, 1/2 c. 15-20
carrots, cooked, 1/2 c. 25-30
cauliflower, 1/2 c. 10-15
corn (kernels), 1/2 c. 70
green beans, 1 c. 30
lettuce, shredded, 1/2 c. 5
mushrooms, canned, 1/2 c. 20
onions, cooked, 1/2 c. 30
peas, cooked, 1/2 c. 60
potato, baked, 1 med. 90
    chips, 8-10 100
    mashed, w/milk & butter, 1 c. ..200-300
spinach, 1 c. 40
tomato, raw, 1 med. 25
    cooked, 1/2 c. 30

COOKING TERMS

Au gratin: Topped with crumbs and/or cheese and browned in oven or under broiler.

Au jus: Served in its own juices.

Baste: To moisten foods during cooking with pan drippings or special sauce in order to add flavor and prevent drying.

Bisque: A thick cream soup.

Blanch: To immerse in rapidly boiling water and allow to cook slightly.

Cream: To soften a fat, especially butter, by beating it at room temperature. Butter and sugar are often creamed together, making a smooth, soft paste.

Crimp: To seal the edges of a two-crust pie either by pinching them at intervals with the fingers or by pressing them together with the tines of a fork.

Crudites: An assortment of raw vegetables (i.e. carrots, broccoli, celery, mushrooms) that is served as an hors d'oeuvre, often accompanied by a dip.

Degrease: To remove fat from the surface of stews, soups or stock. Usually cooled in the refrigerator so that fat hardens and is easily removed.

Dredge: To coat lightly with flour, cornmeal, etc.

Entree: The main course.

Fold: To incorporate a delicate substance, such as whipped cream or beaten egg whites, into another substance without releasing air bubbles. A spatula is used to gently bring part of the mixture from the bottom of the bowl to the top. The process is repeated, while slowly rotating the bowl, until the ingredients are thoroughly blended.

Glaze: To cover with a glossy coating, such as a melted and somewhat diluted jelly for fruit desserts.

Julienne: To cut or slice vegetables, fruits or cheeses into match-shaped slivers.

Marinate: To allow food to stand in a liquid in order to tenderize or to add flavor.

Meuniére: Dredged with flour and sautéed in butter.

Mince: To chop food into very small pieces.

Parboil: To boil until partially cooked; to blanch. Usually final cooking in a seasoned sauce follows this procedure.

Pare: To remove the outermost skin of a fruit or vegetable.

Poach: To cook gently in hot liquid kept just below the boiling point.

Purée: To mash foods by hand by rubbing through a sieve or food mill, or by whirling in a blender or food processor until perfectly smooth.

Refresh: To run cold water over food that has been parboiled in order to stop the cooking process quickly.

Sauté: To cook and/or brown food in a small quantity of hot shortening.

Scald: To heat to just below the boiling point, when tiny bubbles appear at the edge of the saucepan.

Simmer: To cook in liquid just below the boiling point. The surface of the liquid should be barely moving, broken from time to time by slowly rising bubbles.

Steep: To let food stand in hot liquid in order to extract or to enhance flavor, like tea in hot water or poached fruit in syrup.

Toss: To combine ingredients with a repeated lifting motion.

Whip: To beat rapidly in order to incorporate air and produce expansion, as in heavy cream or egg whites.

Publish your own Cookbook

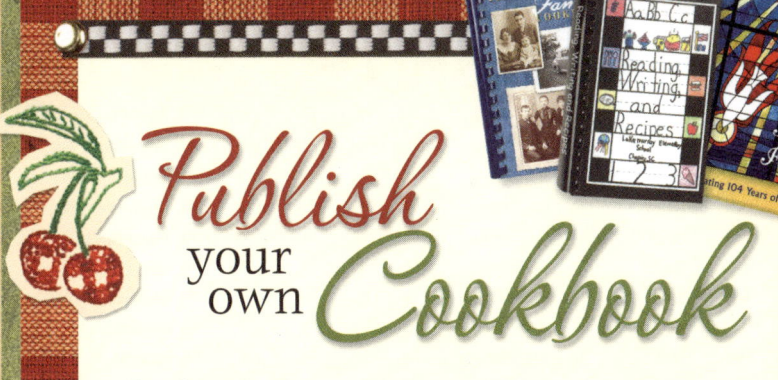

Churches, schools, organizations, and families can preserve their favorite recipes by publishing a custom cookbook. Cookbooks make a great **fundraiser** because they are easy to sell and highly profitable. Our low prices also make cookbooks a perfect affordable **keepsake**. We offer:

- Low prices, high quality, and prompt service.
- Many options and styles to suit your needs.
- 90 days to pay and a written No-Risk Guarantee.

Order our FREE Cookbook Kit for full details:

- Call us at **800-445-6621, ext. CB**.
- Visit our web site at **www.morriscookbooks.com**.
- Mail the **postage-paid reply card** below.

Discover the right ingredients for a really great cookbook!

Order our **FREE** Cookbook Kit. Please print neatly.

Name _____

Organization _____

Address _____

City _____ State _____ Zip _____

E-mail _____

Phone (_____)_____

Back Card 8-09

P. O. Box 2110
Kearney, NE 68848

MORRIS PRESS COOKBOOKS

You supply the recipes and we'll do the rest!™

Publish Your Own Cookbook

Whether your goal is to raise funds or simply create a cherished keepsake, Morris Press Cookbooks has all the right ingredients to make a great custom cookbook. Raise $500–$50,000 while preserving favorite recipes.

You supply the recipes & we'll do the rest!™

Three ways to order our **FREE** Cookbook Kit:
- Call us at **800-445-6621, ext. CB**.
- Visit our web site at **www.morriscookbooks.com**.
- Complete and mail the **postage-paid reply card** below.

BUSINESS REPLY MAIL
FIRST-CLASS MAIL   PERMIT NO. 36   KEARNEY, NE

POSTAGE WILL BE PAID BY ADDRESSEE

NO POSTAGE NECESSARY IF MAILED IN THE UNITED STATES

Morris Press Cookbooks
P.O. Box 2110
Kearney, NE 68848-9985